D1127561

# SLAVERY: A COMPARATIVE PERSPECTIVE

# SLAVERY: A COMPARATIVE PERSPECTIVE

Readings on Slavery
from Ancient Times to the Present

Edited by
Robin W. Winks
*Yale University*

New York: New York University Press
1972

Library of Congress Catalog Card Number: 72-84386
ISBN: 8147-9156-5 (cloth)
8147-9156-3 (paper)

Manufactured in the United States of America

To my Parents

# ACKNOWLEDGMENTS

"The Extent of Slavery" from "Slavery" by Moses I. Finley. Reprinted with permission of the Publisher from the INTERNATIONAL ENCYCLOPEDIA OF THE SOCIAL SCIENCES, David L. Sills, Editor. Volume 14, pages 307-313. Copyright © 1968 by Crowell Collier and Macmillan, Inc.

"Racial Thought and Colonial America" by Louis Ruchames. Reprinted with permission of the Publisher from *The Journal of Negro History*, Vol. 52 (October 1967), pages 251-258, 260-266. Copyright © The Association for the Study of Negro Life and History, Inc.

"Slavery in the West Indies" from "The Origin of Negro Slavery," Chapter I in *Capitalism and Slavery* by Eric Williams. Published by The University of North Carolina Press, 1944. Reprinted by permission of the publisher.

"The Southern Labor System" from "The Origins of Negro Slavery," Chapter 1, pages 3-28 in *Race and Nationality in American Life* by Oscar and Mary F. Handlin. Copyright © by Oscar Handlin. Reprinted by permission of Atlantic-Little, Brown and Co. and Collins-Knowlton-Wing, Inc.

"Debt Bondage in Malaya" by John M. Gullick. Reprinted by permission of The Athelone Press of The University of London.

"New World Systems" from *Slave and Citizen: The Negro in America* by Frank Tannenbaum. Pages 43, 52-63, 65-69. Copyright 1946 by Alfred A. Knopf, Inc. Reprinted by permission of the publisher.

"Prejudice and Slavery" by Carl Degler. Reprinted with permission of The Cambridge University Press from "Slavery and the Genesis of American Race Prejudice," *Comparative Studies in Society and History*, Vol. II, pages 52-62, 66.

"Cuba and Virginia Compared" from *Slavery in the Americas: A Comparative Study of Cuba and Virginia* by Herbert S. Klein. Pages 254-260. Copyright 1967 by The University of Chicago Press. Reprinted by permission of the publisher.

"The Plantation as a Concentration Camp" from *Slavery, A Problem in Institutional and Intellectual Life* by Stanley M. Elkins. Pages 86-89, 115-138. Copyright 1968 by The University of Chicago Press. Reprinted by permission of the publisher.

"Slavery Amongst the Muslims of Africa" from *Slavery and the Muslim Society in Africa* by Allan G. B. and Humphrey J. Fisher. Copyright © 1970 by Allan G. B. Fisher and Humphrey J. Fisher. Reprinted by permission of Doubleday & Company, Inc.

"Brazilian Slavery Examined" from *Vassouras: A Brazilian Coffee County, 1850-1900* by Stanley Stein. Reprinted by permission of Harvard University Press.

"The Myth of the Friendly Master" from *Patterns of Race in America* by Marvin Harris. Copyright © by Walker and Company, New York. Reprinted by permission of the publisher.

"Caribbean Race Relations" from *The Two Variants in Caribbean Race Relations: A Contribution to the Sociology of Segmented Societies* by H. Hoetink. Pages 21-25, 34-35, 74. Published for the Institute of Race Relations, London, by the Oxford University Press. Copyright © by the Institute of Race Relations, 1967.

"Absentee Ownership in the West Indies" from *The Sociology of Slavery* by Orlando Patterson. Reprinted by permission of Granada Publishing Limited and Associated University Presses, Inc.

"A Marxist View of Black Labor" from "The Negro Laborer in Africa and the Slave South" in *The Political Economy of Slavery* by Eugene Genovese. Pages 70-81, 82-84. Copyright © 1960 by *Phylon*, The Atlanta University Review of Race and Culture. Copyright © 1965 by Eugene Genovese. Reprinted by permission of Pantheon Books, a Division of Random House.

"Slavery among the Indians of North America" from *Slavery among the Indians of North America* by IU. P. Averkieva, translated by G. R. Elliott. Reprinted by permission of G. R. Elliott.

"Slavery in Africa" from *Black Mother: The Years of the African Slave Trade* by Basil Davidson. Pages 11-21. Copyright © 1961 by Basil Davidson. Reprinted by permission of Atlantic-Little Brown and Co. and Victor Gollancz Ltd.

"Slavery in the Straits Settlements" from *The Malay States, 1877-1895*. Pages 183-199. Reprinted by permission of Oxford University Press.

"Involuntary Labor since Abolition" from *Involuntary Labour since the Abolition of Slavery: A Survey of Compulsory Labour throughout the World*. Reprinted by permission of N. V. Boekhandel en Drukkerij v/h E. J. Brill.

# CONTENTS

# INTRODUCTION

Slavery has recently become a subject of intense scholarly and some general interest. Concern for the condition of the Negro in modern America, the rise of black militancy, and a renewed desire for compassion in historical judgment are leading many thoughtful Americans to reconsider and ask new questions of a past once thought put to rest. What was slavery? How did it affect the black and the white, and their interactions? Today we are beginning to approach these and other questions with the sophistication they demand and to realize that they are relevant not alone for American or British imperial history, but for an understanding of the broader history of attitudes and beliefs within which slavery has existed.

Recent scholarship has emphasized the patterns of continuity in the history of slavery,[1] and has thus underlined the realization that its "peculiar condition" was neither peculiar nor unique to the New World. During the abolitionist controversy of the nineteenth century, in both Britain and the United States, slavery was said to be unusual, against nature, and against nature's God. It was quite possibly against nature's God, but it was not unusual wherever supporting economic circumstances existed. We have also become increasingly more aware that systems of slavery were far more complex than earlier research had revealed and that easy assumptions about how slave systems differed do not stand up under close scrutiny.

As scholars have come to recognize the many advantages to be gained from taking a comparative perspective upon institutions too often studied within a national framework, they have given ever greater attention to slavery as perhaps an indication both of the cultural values upon which a dominant people bases its attitude toward those subservient within its culture, and of the variety of effects which differing economic, geographic, and ethnic circumstances might have on a seemingly intransigent institution. In short, together with comparative studies of nationalisms and of revolutions, comparative slavery studies have become central to understanding much more than the racial experience alone.

New questions are being asked today, and new controversies have arisen, to which the undergraduate student of history needs an introduction at the very start, since the issues behind the controversies, and on occasion the methods used to explore them, have colored other fields of inquiry. May one study slavery as a problem in American institutional and intellectual life by analogy, for example, as Stanley M. Elkins did? Published in 1959, Elkins' book—which draws comparisons between the concentration camps of Nazi Germany and the regimen of the Southern plantation economy, and uses insights derived from sociology and social phychology—completely reoriented the scholar's approach to slavery. Now under heavy attack,[2] Elkins' work is to be compared with an earlier approach introduced by Frank Tannenbaum in his book *Slave and Citizen*, published in 1947. Tannenbaum explored various slave systems and argued that slavery in Spanish and Portuguese territories, for example, differed substantially from slavery as practiced in British colonies and the American states. Tannenbaum and Elkins have become so widely known and have provoked so much historical revisionist work that their arguments may now be taken to be the primary documents of a new range of historical controversy.

Only now are scholars returning to the truly fundamental questions related to slavery: Did slavery arise because of, rather than in spite of the greater freedom of movement provided by the emergence of the Liberal State? Did not slavery and freedom grow together, the one necessary to the other? Did not the rapid growth of American individualism owe much to the presence of an enslaved labor force? In short, is not slavery based upon racial distinctions only one manifestation of the total problem of slavery? While slavery took on many social and racial meanings, was it not essentially a problem in the supply of labor? If we accept this premise, we must once again wrestle with such questions as Did slavery pay? [3] Under what economic conditions does slavery obtain? [4] Thus, what economic changes are needed in society to remove the need (if, indeed, it can be removed) for involuntary, nonpenal forms of labor?

As suggested, the question of land utilization, the prevalent technology at the time new land was being put to use, and the nature of the available labor supply, as well as the density of population, are basic to an understanding of slavery. As long ago as 1834, when Edward Gibbon Wakefield wrote his *Letter from Sydney*, which was a systematic *View of the Art of Colonization,* industrial societies had begun to wrestle with the problem of how to rationalize a labor supply that had been gained, more often than not, through some form of coercion. While Wakefield's primary interest lay in the systematic settlement of Australia and New Zealand, he saw the relationship between "free land" and social institutions in a way which Frederick Jackson Turner would relate to American history only in 1893, in his famous thesis on the Significance of the Frontier in American History. In that same year Achille Loria, whose earlier work Turner had read, would publish *Les Bases économiques de la constitution sociale*. In 1900, a Dutch scholar, H. J. Nieboer, published his *Slavery as an Industrial System: Ethnological Researches* in The Hague. These scholars saw slavery as an economic question which was related to other aspects of human activity.

The points to be made here, in bringing together this collection of readings, are these: that for too long American historians have been content to examine American slavery as a unique phenomena, and that only in the last two decades have they broken from the American tendency toward exceptionalism, toward assuming that most and perhaps all aspects of the American story were unique rather than a modification of the general Western or even Western European record; that slavery and racism have often been treated as though they were the same problem, where patently they are not, although they are interrelated; that concern with the legal definition of slavery has led scholars to neglect the broader problem of servitude of an involuntary nature, in preindustrial as well as industrial societies; that comparisons between slave systems induced by Western Europeans in the New World represent an important modification of the earlier compartmentalized studies, but that scholars must go further afield to examine, for example, Muslim slavery in Africa, debt-bondage in Malaya, or enforced-labor systems in China or the Soviet Union. To do so is not to strip slavery of the problem of racism, which is basic to an understanding of slave systems, especially in the New World, but it is to show that those who wish to understand slavery must be at once economic and intellectual historians.

Happily, within the last few years studies which take up the questions posed here have begun to appear. The development of Black Studies in American universities has provided a renewed impetus to the comparative study of slave systems. Eugene Genovese, Carl Degler, David Brion Davis, and Winthrop D. Jordan have published significant new work (cited in the bibliographical essay at the end of this volume) which recognizes the complex intertwinings of these many problems. C. Vann Woodward, the leading American scholar of the New South, and Edmund S. Morgan, a leading Colonialist, have begun major new reinterpretations based upon the insights provided by Karl Weber, Nieboer, Willemina Kloosterboer, and others.

There are no collections of readings which will introduce the undergraduate student to the parameters of these new debates, however. To be sure, there are two excellent collections, and the present one in no way displaces these. Richard D. Brown, in *Slavery in American Society*, one of the Problems in American Civilization series published by D. C. Heath (Boston, 1969), provides an excellent overview of New World slavery, with heavy emphasis on North America and the Caribbean. Eugene Genovese and Laura Foner have edited a superb collection of highly sophisticated materials, linked by interpretations of their own, in *Slavery in the New World: A Reader in Comparative History* (Englewood Cliffs, N. J., 1969), published by Prentice-Hall, Inc. As fine as both of these collections are, however, they do not attempt to deal with slavery elsewhere or at other times. The present collection, therefore, is meant to meet a real and growing need for those students who are interested in slavery per se, rather than in its more precise manifestations within the context of a single country or group of countries. The selections used here are more far-ranging, yet often less complex, than those employed by Brown or Genovese and Foner, for the purpose of this volume is to set before the reader a number of broad problems relating to how men, of whatever race and time, have compelled other men to do their bidding, within the context of labor.

Even so, this collection of extracts and essays cannot attempt to present the many questions now being asked about slavery. It is limited to a variety of interpretations on the answers already given to three central questions: Where did slavery exist and why? In what ways did slave systems differ one from another? Are there other forms of servitude which should be viewed within the general perspective of slavery? The short note on additional works should lead the reader on in his exploration of these questions.

Each of the essays printed here may best be read in their fuller contexts, of course, and the reader is urged to turn to the original. All omissions are indicated by an ellipsis. Most footnotes which appeared in the original are omitted, and those retained have been renumbered accordingly; all notes were changed to conform to a single method of citation. Notes inserted by the editor are so shown. While subtitles and other interior divisions have been eliminated from the original selections, no other changes have been made except for those appearing in brackets.

Robin W. Winks

NOTES

1. See, in particular, David Brion Davis, *The Problem of Slavery in Western Culture* (Ithaca, N. Y., 1966).

2. See Ann J. Lane, ed., *The Debate over Slavery: Stanley Elkins and His Critics* (Urbana, Ill., 1971).
3. See Hugh G. J. Aitken, ed., *Did Slavery Pay?: Readings in the Economics of Black Slavery in the United States* (Boston, 1971).
4. This question has been presented and answered most succinctly by Professor W. E. Minchinton of the University of Exeter, in England, in an as yet unpublished paper.

*part one*

# *THE ORIGINS OF SLAVERY*

# 1

# THE EXTENT OF SLAVERY

Slavery has existed since antiquity and in virtually all parts of the world. In terms of service, conditions of work, legal status, and terminology the institution has, of course, differed widely from place to place and from century to century. Plato, Aristotle, Sir Thomas More, and Hegel (in his *Phenomenology*) have written about slavery as both an abstraction and, less often, as a condition. Not only Greece and Rome, but ancient Africa, India, the Muslim world, and the Chinese were familiar with slavery. In the following essay M. I. Finley (1912-     ) of Jesus College, Cambridge, an authority on ancient slavery, explores the range of slave institutions and poses some of the persistent problems.

In classical Roman law, slavery was defined as an institution "whereby someone is subject to the *dominium* of another contrary to nature" . . . *Dominium* can be translated as "power," but the idea of property is also implied. This definition may be accepted as universally applicable without the controversial phrase, "contrary to nature." Distinctions then have to be drawn according to the owner (whether an individual, a corporate institution, the state, or a god), according to the existence or nonexistence of certain "rights" of the slave (such as the claim to eventual manumission, or statutory freedom), and according to the social structure within which slavery functioned. However, the property element remains essential. All forms of labor on behalf of another, whether "free" or "unfree," place the man who labors in the power of another; what separates the slave from the rest, including the serf or peon, is the totality of his powerlessness in principle, and for that the idea of property is juristically the key —hence the term "chattel slave."

For a sociological analysis, however, equal stress must be given to the slave's deracination. The law may declare him, in a formal way, powerless and rightless: one reason the law is enforceable is that he lacks any counterweight or support, whether from a religious institution, from a kinship, group, from his own state or nation, or even from other depressed groups within the society in which he has become a slave. Legally he is not a person. Yet he *is* a human being, and therefore a purely juristic analysis in terms of property, though necessary, is not sufficient.

Conceptually, every man has available to him, or is denied, a bundle of rights and obligations as diverse as freedom of movement, the right to the fruits of his labor, the right to marry and establish a family, the obligation (or right) of military service, the right to look after his soul. It is not normally the case that a man possesses either all of them or none; hence the range and variety of personal statuses found in different societies, and, within limits, even inside a single society, are very considerable. One may speak of a spectrum of statuses between the two extremes of absolute rightlessness and of absolute freedom to exercise all rights at all times. . . . The latter has never existed, nor has the former, although the position of the slave in the American South came very near to it. In between the two extremes, precisely as in a spectrum, there is much shading and overlapping, which the servile vocabulary reflects.

Within the spectrum there are lines of demarcation. Throughout most of human history, labor for others has been performed in large part under conditions of dependence or bondage; that is to say, the relation between the man who works and his master or employer rested neither on ties of kinship nor on a voluntary, revocable contract of employment, but rather on birth into a class of dependents, on debt, or on some other precondition which by custom and law automatically removed from the dependent, usually for a long term or for life, some measure of his freedom of choice and action. "The concept of labor as a salable commodity, apart from the person of the seller, is relatively recent in the history of civilization. . . . In all societies in which dependent labor is common, regardless of the variations within that broad class of persons, one main demarcation line is between the dependents and the others.

Slavery is a species of dependent labor and not the genus. Slaves were to be found in many societies in which other kinds of dependent labor—debt bondsmen, clients, helots, serfs, Babylonian *mushkenū*, Chinese *k'o*, Indian Sudras—were common, just as they coexisted with free labor, However, slavery attained its greatest functional significance, and usually is greatest numerical strength, in societies in which other, less total varieties of bondage had either disappeared or had never existed. The distinction is particularly sharp as between *genuine* slave societies—classical Greece (except Sparta) and Rome, the American South and the Caribbean—on the one hand, and *slave-owning* societies as found in the ancient Near East (including Egypt), India, or China, on the other hand. Only when slaves became the main dependent labor force was the concept of personal freedom first articulated (in classical Greece), and words were then created or adapted to express that idea. It is literally impossible to translate the word "freedom" directly into ancient Babylonian or classical Chinese, and modern European languages cannot render *mushkenum* or *k'o*.

## The slave as outsider

Speculations about the origins of slavery have tended to overlook the specific character of slavery within the broader category of dependent labor. . . .

The slave is an outsider: that alone permits not only his

uprooting but also his reduction from a person to a thing which can be owned. Insiders en masse cannot be so totally transformed; no community could survive that. Thus, free Greeks who wished to dispose of unwanted children were compelled to resort to the fiction that they had "exposed" them (that is, abandoned them in a deserted place); the earliest Roman law code explicitly provided that if a Roman were subject to enslavement as a punishment, he had to be sold abroad . . . , Islamic law always laid down, and usually enforced, the rule that no born Muslim could be enslaved.

Any hypothesis about the origins of slavery must therefore explain how and why a given society turned to outsiders either to supplement or to replace its existing labor force. Supplementation on a small scale, such as the retention of female captives, seems both very ancient and very widespread and presents no analytical problems. But the shift to slavery in a fundamental sense, as a substantial labor force employed in production, is a radical step. The explanations cannot be identical in all instances, because of profound differences in the social structures and economic systems. However, there were always present not only a sufficient material and technical level and a concentration of power which made possible safe procurement of outsiders in sufficient numbers but also the failure, unacceptability, or unavailability of other kinds of labor.

The trauma of enslavement, often entailing great physical suffering as well as severe psychological damage, set up a chain reaction in the behavior of both the slaves and their masters, in which the potential or actual employment of naked force was a permanent and inescapable factor. . . . These behavior patterns and their underlying psychology were reinforced by the slave's lack of essential human ties of kin and community. Free sexual access to slaves marks them off from all other persons as much as their juridical classification as property. On the other hand, not all societies went as far as the American South in the absolute denial to the slave of a *de facto* family of his own. There slavery was complete, so to speak, and the slave's deprivation was extended to the next generation; he lost all control not only over his productive activity but also over his reproduction. In consequence, being born into slavery meant being born an outsider, too.

Prejudice. Prejudices of color, race, nationality, and religion were deeply involved in slavery, not only as ideological justification but also as influences on its institutional development. "Slavery was not born of racism," writes [Eric] Williams * . . . , "rather, racism was the consequence of slavery." However, the question must be asked whether the very idea of enslavement could have been thought of without the extreme distinction between groups, and therefore prejudice, in which "race" in a very loose sense was the criterion. To be sure, Greeks enslaved Greeks from other city-states, for example, and religious conversion, whether to Christianity or to Islam, did not normally release a slave. Nor did community solidarity always prevent penal bondage from sliding into genuine slavery. . . . These are minor aberrations, however. If one could compile statistics of the number of slaves throughout history according to their origins, the proportion of racial, national, and religious outsiders would be overwhelming. Prejudice was certainly an important factor in the Southern American colonies when they decreed, in the 1660s, that henceforth all Negroes, but no whites, who were imported should be slaves and not indentured servants.

Prejudice had its limits, however. For example, it never interfered with sexual relations. It allowed Portuguese officials and missionaries to condone Negro slavery in Brazil while they struggled energetically to emancipate the Amerindians. . . . Slaves drawn from culturally advanced peoples, such as the Hellenized Syrians in Rome, were regularly employed in such occupations as medicine and education. The most remarkable groups of elite slaves—the Mamelukes and Janissaries—illustrate all aspects of the slave outsider. In each generation the Mamelukes were purchased as children outside Islam, were given a rigorous and lengthy religious and military training, and were freed when ready for mili-

---

* West Indian-born scholar, author of *Capitalism and Slavery* (Chapel Hill, N.C., 1944), and Prime Minister of Trinidad and Tobago. (Editor's note.)

tary service. A closed corps was thus created; their only ties were to themselves and their patron (ex-owner), and their elite position was not transmissible to their own children. . , .

## Slave supply

The procurement of a continuous and numerous supply of slaves depended above all on warfare. In early and simple societies, that usually meant raids by the slave-owning society on its source of supply. Even under more advanced conditions, when societies of more or less equal power and culture adjoined each other, regular warfare and raiding may also have been stimulated, at least in part, by the desire for slaves. However, greater stability of supply and greater numbers were ensured in the New World and even to a considerable extent in ancient and medieval times by a more indirect link with war. Neither Portugal nor England made war regularly in Africa in order to meet the demand in the Americas for slaves. The initial act of capture was left to the Africans themselves or to so-called pirates, as it had been left in antiquity to Scythians, Phrygians, and others. In short, the active cooperation of "native" chieftains and tribesmen was critical, and equally so was the role of professional slave traders as the middlemen.

Slave traders often appear as ambiguous figures. The Southern judge who wrote that "the calling of a slavetrader was always hateful, odious, even among slaveholders themselves" . . . was expressing one common judgment, but not the only one, for in England at the same time "his business was a recognized road to gentility". . . . In all countries his financial and governmental backers and his customers were thoroughly "respectable" figures in the community, and the high value of his services was always acknowledged. The suggestion that for a century or more the Roman Senate made no serious effort to suppress piracy in the eastern Mediterranean is probably sound, just as there can be little doubt about influential, though not unchallenged, support for the extensive illicit trade in slaves which followed British abolition after the Napoleonic Wars.

After warfare, breeding was the major source of supply. This is a subject on which much research remains to be done, the results of which will probably confirm the view that no simple generalization is possible. Certainly the often cited "law" that a slave population never reproduces itself is fictitious. In the United States the slaves did better than that, providing a very considerable increase. The question is intimately bound up with many social and economic factors and not with supposedly necessary demographic consequences (biological or otherwise) of the slave status. At one extreme there were conditions such as prevailed in the silvermining district of Athens, where the slaves were almost all males and therefore could not reproduce themselves. At the other extreme there was the systematic, profitable breeding in the poorer regions of the American South. . . . In between these extremes, there was a great range of possibilities, conditioned by, among other things, the prevailing rules regarding the inheritance of slave status. These rules appear bewildering in their variety, but much the commonest was that the child took the mother's status.

## The uses of slaves

The actual numbers of slaves in any society are rarely known. The American South provides the decisive exception, and there the figures show an upper limit far below the often repeated exaggerations, such as the 400,000 claimed for ancient Athens. In 1860 slightly fewer than one-third of the population of the American slave states were slaves. Furthermore, "nearly three-fourths of all free Southerners had no connection with slavery through either family ties or direct ownership. The 'typical' Southerner was not only a small farmer but also a nonslaveholder." . . . What counts in evaluating the place of slavery in any society is, therefore, not absolute totals or proportions, but rather *location* and *function*. If the economic and political elite depended primarily on slave labor for basic production, then one may speak of a slave society. It does not matter, in such situations, whether as many as three-fourths were not slaveholders, or whether slavery was fairly widespread outside the elite in domestic or other nonproductive roles.

Wherever there are slaves, they will be found in domestic (and therefore also sexual) roles. Such roles have their own spectrum, ranging from the "drawers of water" and meanest prostitutes to domestics who were occupationally employed by their craftsmen-owners and to eunuchal grand viziers and harem favorites. If, however, this is the social location of most of the slaves, then it must follow that other kinds of dependent (or, on occasion, free) labor together with independent peasants and craftsmen constitute the productive labor force. That was the case in the ancient Near East, China, India, and medieval Europe and Byzantium as well as the Islamic world of the same period, and it is still the case in Saudi Arabia.

The economics of slavery. Slavery, then, is transformed as an institution when slaves play an essential role in the economy. Historically that has meant, in the first instance, their role in agriculture. Slavery has been accommodated to the large estate under radically different conditions: the Roman latifundia did not practice the monoculture of the modern plantation, and they existed within an essentially precapitalist economy. However, both types of estate produced for the market, and they both existed alongside widespread free small holding. That both slaves and free men did identical work was irrelevant; what mattered was the condition of the work, or rather, on whose behalf and under what (and whose) controls it was carried on. In slave societies hired labor was rare and slave labor the rule whenever an enterprise was too big for a family to conduct unaided. That rule extended from agriculture to manufacture and mining, and sometimes even to commerce and finance. . . . A number of variables are involved: the poverty of the soil, as in Athens and other Greek cities; the special position of a particular region within an international network of economic relations, as in the American South; or the special role of the state as a large consumer of manufactures, as in the later Roman and Byzantine empires.

As an economic institution, slavery was "profitable"; this can be asserted with confidence, despite frequent attempts to deny it. In the strict sense of the term, the question of profitability does not enter into an evaluation of domestic slaves, court eunuchs and concubines, or Mamelukes. Nor is there any value in hypothetical arguments about whether or not Roman senators could have managed their latifundia even more profitably with some other kind of labor force. They made very large fortunes for centuries on end, and there is no other way to calculate the economics of slavery in a precapitalist society. As for the American South, it can no longer be seriously questioned that slave plantations were profitable "in a strict accounting sense" . . . , whatever the effects of slavery on further economic growth within a competitive world economy. In the accounting, it is important to give proper weight to the profitability of slave breeding in the agriculturally poorer regions. In addition, there were the profits of the slave trade, which might or might not accrue to members of the slaveholding society itself.

## Slaves and masters

The difficulties in properly understanding the personality and the psychology of the slave are obvious. Neither the remarks by contemporary writers (whether slaveholders or outside reporters) nor the relatively few documents emanating from slaves themselves can be taken at face value. Yet a special slave psychology must have developed (speaking in group terms, of course). In order to survive as human beings, slaves had to adapt to their new state of deracination by developing new psychological features and new focuses of attachment, including their overseers and masters. Slave elites, whether individual overseers or whole groups of slaves and freedmen (ex-slaves), such as the imperial *familia* in Rome or the Mamelukes in Egypt, serve to exemplify how far adaptation and acceptance could be pushed under certain conditions. The slave-type—the celever schemer of Greek and Roman comedy or the childlike, indolent, amoral Sambo familiar to American literature and popular humor—is no doubt a stereotype and a caricature, but, . . . it cannot be a pure invention out of nothing.

Slave rebellions. The slave was a "troublesome property." . . . In its most extreme form, "being troublesome" meant revolt, but large-scale revolt is extremely difficult to organize and has, in fact, been a relatively rare phenomenon in the history of slavery. Throughout classical antiquity there were only three revolts of any mark, each involving 100,000 or more slaves, and all concentrated within the short time span of 135-70 B.C. Common to all three were the presence of certain necessary conditions, including a severe breakdown of the social order and the concentration of large numbers of slaves with common nationality, language, and culture, among them men with unusual potentialities of leadership. . . . It is important to contrast the ancient chattel slaves with the helots (in Sparta and elsewhere) in this respect: the latter were permanently mutinous in an organized way, presumably because they belonged to a class of dependent labor which retained the normal human ties of solidarity with kin and community. The Caribbean throughout the eighteenth and early nineteenth centuries was also an area of persistent revolt. In the United States, under conditions which differed above all by being noncolonial, not a single serious revolt ever occurred; for example, the "Turner cataclysm" of 1831 was a purely local affair lasting a few months from its inception (with only three days of actual fighting) and involving only some hundreds of men. . . .

"Being troublesome," in sum, usually meant something much less than outright rebellion, such as flight, sabotage, theft, and inefficiency. None of these is expressible in quantitative terms or easy to evaluate. There is American evidence to support the famous judgment of the economist [John E.] Cairnes (1862) that slave labor was on the lowest level of skill because slaves were both uneducated and uncooperative. . . . On the other hand, the possibilties of "loyalty," which is equally immeasurable, cannot be ignored. In contrast to American slaves, the slaves of ancient Greece and Rome were regularly and successfully employed in the most highly skilled occupations. Relative mildness or harshness of treatment cannot be a sufficient explanation of such variations, which must lie deep in the social structure and in psychology. Likewise, variations in the practice of manumission, in the place of freedmen in the society, and in the accompanying psychology require complex explanations.

Attitudes of the masters. In the ancient world the institution of slavery was never challenged, despite the notion that it was "contrary to nature." No serious argument was ever put forward for the abolition of slavery in ancient Greece and Rome (as distinct from relative liberality in freeing individual slaves), on moral or any other grounds; this was also the case in India, China, and the Islamic world. Nor did Christianity change the fundamental attitude after it became the official and more or less universal religion of both the western and eastern halves of the Roman Empire. Slavery declined sharply at the end of antiquity, but for reasons having nothing to do with moral ideas. Furthermore, it was in the Christian states in southern and southwestern Europe that slavery was considerably revived in the late Middle Ages . . . , and it was among the Christian conquerors of the New World that it received its newest and most vigorous re-creation. Paradoxically, it was then that the most powerful and persistent claims were put forward for the "naturalness" of slavery, with ample quotation from the Bible, and that moral arguments for the *abolition* of slavery were fully mustered for the first time.

The whole subject of the psychological effects of slavery calls urgently for further investigation—from the side of the masters (including the free poor who themselves owned no slaves) as well as from the side of the slaves. The need to be brutal, ideologically as well as physically, must have had repercussions on the master's psyche. The easy sexual access to slave women influenced all attitudes toward sex and women: witness the quasi-chivalric ideology of Southern womanhood. Furthermore, the identification of certain forms of physical labor with slavery, including the essential labor in agriculture, had its effects on the free man's choice of employment and on his spirit of enterprise generally. More often than not, the majority of free farmers and craftsmen, out of necessity, performed labor similar to that of the slave. Even then, however, there were subtle effects on the direction into which creative talents and energies were channeled, and there were certain employments into which it was extremely difficult to move the free poor when they were needed. Policy makers in underdeveloped countries are still coming up against just such resistance . . . , although it usually follows the abolition of forms of dependent labor other than slavery.

## Slavery and Marxist theory

Marxist theory, by its very nature, has assigned a unique historical position to slavery. History is viewed as a progress through a number of stages, each genetically determined within its predecessor and each founded on a particular mode of production (social relations of production), of which one is slavery. In the past half century, in particular, the way in which historical analysis was enmeshed in, not to say dominated by, current political discussion produced among orthodox Marxists a rigid, universal, unilinear scheme of development in five stages: primitive communism, slavery, feudalism, capitalism, and socialism. Even the ancient Near East and ancient China, it was held, were slave societies, and there were persistent but wholly unsuccessful efforts to discover general laws or general features common to all slave societies.

However, scattered through Marx's writings down to the early 1860s there are also brief, not fully developed references to an "Asiatic mode of production." His only attempt to examine this systematically was in one section of a bulky manuscript written in 1857-1858 but not published until 1939-41 and not widely known before the 1950s. In this sophisticated account, the Asiatic mode of production is characterized as one in which there was no private property in the land and in which a despotic government ruled over the village communities, whose members were in a condition of "general slavery" and who were therefore not slaves in the chattel sense at all. Publication of this work has sparked a very intense new discussion, following a hiatus of nearly a generation. . . . The discussion is still in an early and fluid state, but the general trend seems clear. It is argued that the stages of evolution in European history from which the traditional scheme was constructed do not constitute a model for world history at all but were, on the contrary, a unique development. As a corollary, the "Asiatic" mode of production has been found on other continents as well, for example in Bronze Age Greece and among the Incas. The place of slavery in Marxist theory thus seems to be undergoing a redefinition to fit a multilinear pattern of development.

# 2

# RACIAL THOUGHT AND COLONIAL AMERICA

Did slavery precede racial prejudice, or was it because of racial prejudice that one group, the Black man, ultimately came to comprise most slaves? Did ideas, rather than economic realities, provide the prior justification for slavery? May racism be separated from the economic condition that fostered it? These questions have led to a continuing debate about how white came to dominate black in North America. In the answers would lie solutions to how black might dominate white, or to how both groups might no longer think in terms of dominance at all. Three of the essays here—the one that follows, and those by Oscar and Mary F. Handlin and by Carl Degler—turn upon the question of sequence, of cause and effect relationships, that lies at the heart of all historical inquiry. The first essay is by Louis Ruchames (1917- ), Chairman of the Department of History at the Boston campus of the University of Massachusetts, and a student of American abolitionism. Ruchames has elaborated on the themes given here in his *Racial Thought in America* (Amherst, Mass., 1969).

Racial thought is as old as civilized man. It had its origin in man's first awareness of physical, cultural, religious or economic differences between groups. The explanation of these differences in terms of durable and hereditary group characteristics, physical or mental, constitutes racial as distinct from other forms of explanation.

The racial thoughts, attitudes and prejudices brought to the American continent by the earliest colonists were those that prevailed in Europe in their day. Racial thought had been a part of European and Oriental culture since antiquity. Its elements existed in India, China, Egypt, Palestine and Greece. In the thought of Aristotle, notes Friedrich Hertz, "we find modern race theories sketched in outline."[1] Aristotle propounded the view that some men are destined by nature to be masters and others to be slaves, with each given those qualities appropriate to his position in society. In Aristotle's view, the relationship of master and slave is for their mutual benefit. As he notes in the *Politics*, "It is clear, then, that some men are by nature free, and others slaves, and that for these latter slavery is both expedient and right."

During the Middle Ages and extending into the early modern period, racial thought was used to explain differences between economic and social classes, especially the peasantry and the nobility. Some thinkers regarded the peasants as descended from Ham, the accursed son of Noah, and the knights from the Trojan heroes, who had presumably settled in England, Germany and France after their defeat. In the seventeenth century, Count de Boullainvi[lli]ers, a spokesman of the French nobility, declared the nobility to have been descended from their Germanic conquerors and the masses of the people from the subject Celts and Normans.

Ethnocentrism and slavery were additional elements of the cultural heritage which the early colonists brought to this continent. Slavery had existed in Europe since antiquity. While it declined in Western Europe from about 900 to 1300, giving place to serfdom, it increased again at the end of the Middle Ages and during the early modern period. Venetian and Genoese slave traders bought Armenians, Bulgarians, Circassians and Serbs from the Turks and sold them in Mediterranean countries. Spanish Christians sold Moors into Slavery as they conquered all of Spain. Moslem traders in Africa brought Sudanese Negroes across the Sahara to North African ports and sold them to Mediterranean towns as house slaves. After the fall of Constantinople in 1453, at least 50,000 of the citizens were sold into slavery. As the Portuguese made their discoveries of land and Negroes along the African coast in the fifteenth century, the trade in slaves rose. The voyage of John Hawkins to Guinea in 1562, where he acquired three hundred Negroes, which he then sold in Hispaniola, meant the entrance of England into the slave trade and the beginning of what ultimately became vast increase in the number of Africans who were sold as slaves.

Ethnocentrism provided the rationale and the apology for slavery and the slave trade. Christianity, as the only true religion, and Christians, as the new "chosen People," could do with the earth and its non-Christian populations as they saw fit. Heathens, Jews, Moslems and others were fair game for Christians; witness Pope Nicholas V's order in 1452 empowering the King of Portugal "to despoil and sell into slavery all Moslems, heathen and other foes of Christ." The Church itself held slaves. Moorish slaves sent to Pope Innocent VIII in 1488 by Ferdinand the Catholic were distributed among the Cardinals and other dignitaries. Although, as early as about 600 A.D., Pope Gregory the Great had expressed the opinion that manumission was a great good and had freed two church slaves, the accepted interpretation was that it applied primarily to those who accepted Christianity and even in these instances "manumission was not the right of the slave but a pious and commendable act on the part of the master."

Nor is there any doubt but that slavery was accepted as a necessary social institution by most European thinkers. Two men as different as Sir Thomas More and Martin Luther argued the need for slavery. More included slavery in his Utopia and Luther used the Bible to justify slavery and the sale of slaves. . . .

Slavery and the slave trade received their greatest impetus with the discovery of America and the subsequent effort to exploit its resources of men and materials. The Indians were enslaved on planatations and in mines. Though such humanitarians as the Spanish priest Bartolomé de Las Casas protested against Spanish enslavement of the Indians,[2] and the institution itself was prohibited by royal decree in the famous New Laws of 1542, the prohibition was not always observed by the colonists, and where it was observed, other forms of forced labor took the place of outright slavery. As the Indians of South America were decimated by overwork and disease, Negroes were imported from Africa to take their place. Because of the expensiveness of such importation, the African slave trade did not reach its full stride until the end of the sixteenth century when sugar consumption "skyrocketed," sugar became "the most valuable agricultural commodity in international trade," [3] and the vast profits from sugar production justified the high cost of the African slave trade. The result was the importation of an estimated 900,000 Africans into the New World in the sixteenth century and 2,750,000 in the seventeenth.

With the increase in slavery and the slave trade and more numerous contacts of Europeans with Indians and Negroes, European scholars began to give greater attention to race and racial differences. It is interesting to note that it was only during the modern period that the term "race" came into use. The English term was first used at the beginning of the sixteenth century, the Italian *razza* first appeared in the fourteenth century, while the Spanish *raza*, the Portuguese *raca* and the Frence *race* were first used in the fifteenth century.

Such questions as whether or not Negroes and Indians were to be regarded as human beings whose souls could be saved by conversion to Christianity; the origin of racial differences, especially skin color; and whether or not other races were inferior to whites, began to interest Europeans. At a very early date, "a favorite Spanish theory was to look upon them [the Indians] as descendants of the lost ten tribes of Israel." [4] A Scottish professor in Paris, John Major, first applied Aristotelian doctrine of natural slavery to the Indians in a book published in Paris in 1510. Antonio de Montesinos, a Spanish Dominican friar, preached a sermon in Hispaniola in 1511, in which he protested against Spanish mistreatment of the Indians and asked: "Are these Indians not men? Do they not have rational souls? Are you not obliged to love them as you love yourselves?"

As a result of the efforts of Las Casas and others, who opposed enslavement of the Indians no less than their extermination, Pope Paul III, in 1537, issued a bull entitled "Sublimis Deus." In it he condemned the view that the Indians "should be treated as dumb brutes created for our service . . . incapable of receiving the catholic faith," and affirmed that "the Indians are truly men and that they are not only capable of understanding the catholic faith but, according to our information, they desire exceedingly to receive it." At the same time, he decreed that the Indians "are by no means to be deprived of their liberty or the possession of their property, even though they be outside the faith of Jesus Christ; and that they may and should . . . enjoy their liberty and the possession of their property; nor should they be in any way enslaved. . . ."

One of the important events in the history of racial thought took place in 1550 and 1551 at Valladolid, Spain, in a debate between Juan Genés de Sepulveda and Las Casas, on the question of whether the Aristotelian theory, that some men are slaves by nature, could be applied to the Indians. Sepulveda argued that the Indians were rude and inferior beings by nature, with no capacity for political life, whose inferiority required that the superior Spaniards rule over them. Las Casas argued that the Indians were rational beings, superior to many ancient peoples, even the Greeks and Romans, and therefore worthy of freedom. Neither contestant gained a clear-cut victory. . . .

Other thinkers too were speculating about the nature of races. In 1520, Paracelsus declared that Negroes and other peoples were not descended from Adam, and in 1591, Giordano Bruno maintained that "No sound thinking person will refer the Ethiopians to the same protoplast as the Jewish one." During the same century, Montaigne, who believed in the equality of all men, remarked concerning the Brazilian Indian: "There is nothing savage or barbarous about his nature save for the fact that each of us labels whatever is not among the customs of his own people as barbarism."

During the sixteenth and seventeenth centuries, English opinion of the slave trade and slavery, as well as of Negroes and Indians, was not very different from that of most Spaniards and Portuguese. Most Englishmen approved of slavery and despised Negroes and Indians. To some extent, theory was better than practice. Many Englishmen who had read Las Casas' writings at the end of the century . . . were horrified by Spanish cruelty. There were Englishmen who believed that if placed in a similar situation, they would treat the natives better than did the Spanish. . . .

African Negroes were known to Englishmen primarily through the African slave trade and West Indian plantations. The result, as might be expected, was that Negroes were regarded as inferior beings who were fit only for slavery or a "savage" existence in Africa. The same may be said for English attitudes toward the Indians, which, despite an occasional protesting voice, were best expressed by William Cunningham in 1559, when he spoke of Indians as "comparable to brute beasts."

It was but a short step to the opinion which finally prevailed that the English as civilized and superior human beings, who were Christians and therefore the elect of God, had the right to possess themselves of the territories of the savage Indians, as the Israelites did the lands of the Canaanites. The recompense to the Indians was the opportunity to convert to Christianity and thus to achieve salvation. Indeed, as was true also of the Spanish settlers, the Christianization of the Indians was regarded as a serious responsibility of the settlers by many clergymen as well as laymen and was one of the chief rationalizations of the colonization enterprise. . . . Many, if not most of [Sir Walter] Raleigh's contemporaries, were convinced . . . of "the right of followers of the true Jehovah to take by force the lands of the Canaanites." The most popular arguments for colonization were those that united the saving of souls with material advancement.

. . . This helps to explain the well known if apocryphal story of a meeting of the settlers of Milford, Conn., at which the problem of taking Indians' lands was discussed. The settlers came to a decision which was inscribed in the minutes of their meeting and which took the form of a syllogism.

"1. The earth is the Lord's and the fullness thereof. Voted.

"2. The Lord can dispose of the earth to his saints. Voted.

"3. We are his saints. Voted." [5]

That conversion to Christianity made little difference in the Puritan treatment of Indians, is suggested by Theodore Parker, the great Unitarian scholar: "A sharp distinction was always made," he writes, "between converted Indians and other Christians; they were treated, in every respect, as an inferior race; restricted to villages of their own, and cut off by opinion, as well as law, from intermarriage and intercourse with the whites. No one was allowed to sell them horses or boats. It was proposed to exterminate them, as being of the 'cursed seed of Ham' " . . .

Theodore Parker . . . underscores the sharp racial consciousness of the early settlers. "In New England more pains were taken than elsewhere in America to spare, to civilize, and to convert the sons of the wilderness; but yet here the distinction of race was always sharply observed. Even community of religion and liturgical rites, elsewhere so powerful a bond of union, was unable to soften the Englishman's repugnance to the Indian. The Puritan hoped to meet the Pequods in heaven, but wished to keep apart from them on earth, nay, to exterminate them from the land. Besides, the English met with no civilized tribe in America, and for them to unite in wedlock with such children of the forest as they found in North America would have been contrary, not only to the Anglo-Saxon prejudice, but to the general usage of the world—a usage to which even the French in Canada afford but a trifling exception. The Spaniards had less of this exclusiveness of race, perhaps, none at all. They met with civilized tribes of red men, met and mingled in honorable and permanent connection. In Peru and Mexico, at this day, there are few men of pure Spanish blood."

Parker's opinion that the English colonists showed much greater prejudice toward Indians and Negroes than did the Spanish and Portuguese, is shared by many observers, some of whom apply the distinction to English and French settlers as well. The English seem to have segregated the Indians and Negroes and passed laws prohibiting interracial marriages far more than did the Spanish, the Portuguese or the French. It is also claimed that slavery in Latin America, under the Spanish and Portuguese, was far less severe than among the English in the Southern portion of the United States.

Several explanations have been given for these differing national attitudes toward racial segregation and slavery. They have included differences between Catholic and Protestant theology and religious belief, the influence of Roman law on Spanish and Portuguese slavery, and the longer contact of the Portuguese and the Spanish with colored peoples. . . .

NOTES

1. Friedrich Hertz, *Race and Civilization,* tr. by A. S. Levetus and W. Entz (New York, 1928), p. 4. For examples of racial thought in antiquity, see Thomas F. Gossett, *Race: The History of an Idea* (Dallas, 1963), p. 3 ff. In one instance, Gossett's treatment is tendentious. In delineating the views of the early Hebrews he fails to mention those opposed to racial or religious superiority, as, for example, the books of Ruth and Jonah.
2. For further information about Las Casas see Lewis Hanke, *Bartolomé de Las Casas* (Philadelphia, 1952); Marcel Brion, *Bartolomé de Las Casas* (New York, 1929); Arthur Helps, *Life of Las Casas* (London, 1868). Originally Las Casas favored the introduction of Negro slaves to replace the Indians, believing the former better able to withstand the heavy work demanded by the Spaniards. He later changed his opinion and opposed Negro enslavement as well. . . .

3. Marvin Harris, *Patterns of Race in the Americas* (New York, 1964), p. 13.
4. Woodbury Lowery, *The Spanish Settlements Within the Present Limits of the United States,* 1513-1561 (New York and London), 1901, p. 56.
5. Louis B. Wright, *Religion and Empire: The Alliance between Piety and Commerce in English Expansion, 1558-1625* (Chapel Hill, N.C., 1943), pp. 157-58.

3

# SLAVERY IN THE WEST INDIES

In the New World, slavery began in the West Indies. It soon seemed indispensable to the economy and way of life of the British and French colonies in the Caribbean. The chief need was for guaranteed supplies of labor which would be at once hardy, docile, and numerous. A black historian, Eric Williams (1911- ), explored the relationship between capitalism and slavery in 1944; he concluded that the British abolitionists, and the humanitarianism of the Saints in general, had less to do with the striking down of slavery within the British Empire in 1834 than the humanitarians themselves had thought. Rather, slavery was ceasing to be a useful (i.e., profitable) practice. For this conclusion, Williams was labeled a Marxist historian, although his work is not particularly so, even while being economic in its orientation. The material that follows here deals not with the abolitionists, however, but with the origins of Negro slavery as such. Williams is now the Prime Minister of the independent nation of Trinidad and Tobago, but he continues to write, most recently on how British historians have viewed the history of the West Indies.

Slavery in the Caribbean has been too narrowly identified with the Negro. A racial twist has thereby been given to what is basically an economic phenomenon. Slavery was not born of racism: rather, racism was the consequence of slavery. Unfree labor in the New World was brown, white, black, and yellow; Catholic, Protestant and pagan.

The first instance of slave trading and slave labor developed in the New World involved, racially, not the Negro but the Indian. The Indians rapidly succumbed to the excessive labor demanded of them, the insufficient diet, the white man's diseases, and their inability to adjust themselves to the new way of life. Accustomed to a life of liberty, their constitution and temperament were ill-adapted to the rigors of plantation slavery. As Fernando Ortíz writes: "To subject the Indian to the mines, to their monotonous, insane and severe labor, without tribal sense, without religious ritual, . . . was like taking away from him the meaning of his life. . . . It was to enslave not only his muscles but also his collective spirit."

The visitor to Ciudad Trujillo, capital of the Dominican Republic (the present-day name of half of the island formerly called Hispaniola), will see a statue of Columbus, with the figure of an Indian woman gratefully writing (so reads the caption) the name of the Discoverer. The story is told, on the other hand, of the Indian chieftain, Hatuey, who, doomed to die for resisting the invaders, staunchly refused to accept the Christian faith as the gateway to salvation when he learned that his executioners, too, hoped to get to Heaven. It is far more probable that Hatuey, rather than the anonymous woman, represented contemporary Indian opinion of their new overlords.

England and France, in their colonies, followed the Spanish practice of enslavement of the Indians. There was one conspicuous difference—the attempts of the Spanish Crown, however ineffective, to restrict Indian slavery to those who refused to accept Christianity and to the warlike Caribs on the specious plea that they were cannibals. From the standpoint of the British government Indian slavery, unlike later Negro slavery which involved vital imperial interests, was a purely colonial matter. . . .

. . . Indian slavery never was extensive in the British dominions. . . . In the New England colonies Indian slavery was unprofitable, for slavery of any kind was unprofitable because it was unsuited to the diversified agriculture of these colonies. In addition the Indian slave was inefficient. The Spaniards discovered that one Negro was worth four Indians. A prominent official in Hispaniola insisted in 1518 that "permission be given to bring Negroes, a race robust for labor, instead of natives, so weak that they can only be employed in tasks requiring little endurance, such as taking care of maize fields or farms." The future staples of the New World, sugar and cotton, required strength which the Indian lacked, and demanded the robust "cotton nigger" as sugar's need of strong mules produced in Louisiana the epithet "sugar mules." . . .

The Indian reservoir, too, was limited, the African inexhaustible. Negroes therefore were stolen in Africa to work the lands stolen from the Indians in America. The voyages of Prince Henry the Navigator complemented those of Columbus, West African history became the complement of West Indian.

The immediate successor of the Indian, however, was not the Negro but the poor white. These white servants included a variety of types. Some were indentured servants, so called because, before departure from the homeland, they had signed a contract, indented by law, binding them to service for a stipulated time in return for their passage. Still others, known as "redemptioners," arranged with the captain of the ship to pay for their passage on arrival or within a specified time thereafter; if they did not, they were sold by the captain to the highest bidder. Others were convicts, sent out by the deliberate policy of the home government, to serve for a specified period.

This emigration was in tune with mercantilist theories of the day which strongly advocated putting the poor to industrious and useful labor and favored emigration, voluntary or involuntary, as relieving the poor rates and finding more profitable occupations abroad for idlers and vagrants at home. . . . In a state paper delivered to James I in 1600 [Francis] Bacon emphasized that by emigration England would gain "a double commodity, in the avoidance of people here, and in making use of them there."

This temporary service at the outset denoted no inferiority

or degradation. Many of the servants were manorial tenants fleeing from the irksome restrictions of feudalism, Irishmen seeking freedom from the oppression of landlords and bishops, Germans running away from the devastation of the Thirty Years' War. They transplanted in their hearts a burning desire for land, an ardent passion for independence. They came to the land of opportunity to be free men, their imaginations powerfully wrought upon by glowing and extravagant descriptions in the home country. It was only later when . . . the introduction of disreputable elements became a general feature of indentured service.

A regular traffic developed in these indentured servants. Between 1654 and 1685 ten thousand sailed from Bristol alone, chiefly for the West Indies and Virginia. In 1683 white servants represented one-sixth of Virginia's population. Two-thirds of the immigrants to Pennsylvania during the eighteenth century were white servants; in four years 25,000 came to Philadelphia alone. It has been estimated that more than a quarter of a million persons were of this class during the colonial period, and that they probably constituted one-half of all English immigrants, the majority going to the middle colonies.

As commercial speculation entered the picture, abuses crept in. Kidnaping was encouraged to a great degree and became a regular business in such towns as London and Bristol. Adults would be plied with liquor, children enticed with sweetmeats. The kidnapers were called "spirits," defined as "one that taketh upp men and women and children and sells them on a shipp to be conveyed beyond the sea." The captain of a ship trading to Jamaica would visit the Clerkenwell House of Correction, ply with drink the girls who had been imprisoned there as disorderly, and "invite" them to go to the West Indies. The temptations held out to the unwary and the credulous were so attractive that, as the mayor of Bristol complained, husbands were induced to forsake their wives, wives their husbands, and apprentices their masters, while wanted criminals found on the transport ships a refuge from the arms of the law. The wave of German immigration developed the "newlander," the labor agent of those days, who traveled up and down the Rhine Valley persuading the feudal peasants to sell their belongings and emigrate to America, receiving a commission for each emigrant. . . .

Convicts provided another steady source of white labor. The harsh feudal laws of England recognized three hundred capital crimes. Typical hanging offences included: picking a pocket for more than a shilling; shoplifting to the value of five shillings; stealing a horse or a sheep; poaching rabbits on a gentleman's estate. Offences for which the punishment prescribed by law was transportation comprised the stealing cloth, burning stacks of corn, the maiming and killing of cattle, hindering customs officers in the execution of their duty, and corrupt legal practices. Proposals made in 1664 would have banished to the colonies all vagrants, rogues and idlers, petty thieves, gipsies, and loose persons frequenting unlicensed brothels. . . . One year after the emancipation of the Negro slaves, transportation was the penalty for trade union activity. It is difficult to resist the conclusion that there was some connection between the law and the labor needs of the plantations, and the marvel is that so few people ended up in the colonies overseas.

Benjamin Franklin opposed this "dumping upon the New World of the outcasts of the Old" as the most cruel insult ever offered by one nation to another, and asked, if England was justified in sending her convicts to the colonies, whether the latter were justified in sending to England their rattlesnakes in exchange? It is not clear why Franklin should have been so sensitive. Even if the convicts were hardened criminals, the great increase of indentured servants and free emigrants would have tended to render the convict influence innocuous, as increasing quantities of water poured in a glass containing poison. Without convicts the early development of the Australian colonies in the nineteenth century would have been impossible. Only a few of the colonists, however, were so particular. The general attitude was summed up by a contemporary: "Their labor would be more beneficial in an infant settlement, than their vices could be pernicious." There was nothing strange about this attitude. The great problem in a new country is the problem of labor, and convict labor, as [Herman] Merivale has pointed out, was equivalent to a free present by the government to the settlers without burdening the latter with the expense of importation. . . .

The political and civil disturbances in England between 1640 and 1740 augmented the supply of white servants. Political and religious nonconformists paid for their unorthodoxy by transportation, mostly to the sugar islands. Such was the fate of many of [Oliver] Cromwell's Irish prisoners, who were sent to the West Indies. So thoroughly was this policy pursued that an active verb was added to the English language—to "barbadoes" a person. Montserrat became largely an Irish colony, and the Irish brogue is still frequently heard today in many parts of the British West Indies. The Irish, however, were poor servants. They hated the English, were ways ready to aid England's enemies, and in a revolt in the Leeward Islands in 1689 [5] we can already see signs of that burning indignation which, according to [W. E. H.] Lecky, gave Washington some of his best soldiers. The vanquished in Cromwell's Scottish campaigns were treated like the Irish before them, and Scotsmen came to be regarded as "the general travaillers and soldiers in most foreign parts." Religious intolerance sent more workers to the plantations. In 1661 Quakers refusing to take the oath for the third time were to be transported; in 1664 transportation, to any plantation except Virginia or New England, or a fine of one hundred pounds was decreed for the third offence for persons over sixteen assembling in groups of five or more under pretence of religion. . . .

The transportation of these white servants shows in its true light the horrors of the Middle Passage—not as something unusual or inhuman but as a part of the age. The emigrants were packed like herrings. . . . The boats were small, the voyage long, the food, in the absence of refrigeration, bad, disease inevitable. A petition to Parliament in 1659 describes how seventy-two servants had been locked up below deck during the whole voyage of five and a half weeks, "amongst horses, that their souls, through heat and steam under the tropic, fainted in them. . . .

The transportation of servants and convicts produced a powerful vested interest in England. When the Colonial Board was created in 1661, not the least important of its duties was the control of the trade in indentured servants. In 1664 a commission was appointed, headed by the King's brother, to examine and report upon the exportation of servants. In 1670 an act prohibiting the transportation of English prisoners overseas was rejected; another bill against the stealing of children came to nothing. In the transportation of felons, a whole hierarchy, from courtly secretaries and grave judges down to the jailors and turnkeys, insisted on having a share in the spoils. . . .

. . . The fear of overpopulation at the beginning of the seventeenth century gave way to a fear of underpopulation in the middle of the same century. The essential condition of colonization—emigration from the home country—now ran counter to the principle that national interest demanded a large population at home. Sir Josiah Child denied that emigration to America had weakened England, but he was forced to admit that in his view he was in a minority of possibly one in a thousand, while he endorsed the general opinion that "whatever tends to the depopulating of a kingdom tends to the impoverishment of it. . . . [T]he Royal Family had already given their patronage to the Royal African Company and the Negro slave trade. For the surplus population needed to people the colonies in the New World the British had turned to Africa, and by 1680 they already had positive evidence, in Barbados, that the African was satisfying the necessities of production better than the European.

The status of these servants became progressively worse in the plantation of colonies. Servitude, originally, a free personal relation based on voluntary contract for a definite period of service, in lieu of transportation and maintenance, tended to pass into a property relation which asserted a control of varying extent over the bodies and liberties of the person during service as if he were a thing. . . . In Maryland servitude developed into an institution approaching in some respects chattel slavery. Of Pennsylvania it has been said that "no matter how kindly they may have been treated in particular cases, or how voluntarily they may have entered into the relation, as a class and when once bound, indentured servants were temporarily chattels.". . .

English officialdom . . . took the view that servitude was not too bad, and the servant in Jamaica was better off than the husbandman in England. "It is a place as grateful to you for a trade as any part of the world. It is not so odious as it is represented. But there was some sensitiveness on the question. The Lords of Trade and Plantations, in 1676, opposed the use of the word "servitude" as a mark of bondage and slavery, and suggested "service" instead. The institution was not affected by the change. The hope has been expressed that the white servants were spared the lash so liberally bestowed upon their Negro comrades. They had no such good fortune. Since they were bound for a limited period, the planter had less interest in their welfare than in that of the Negroes who were perpetual servants and therefore "the most useful appurtenances" of a plantation. . . . The servants were regarded by the planters as "white trash," and were bracketed with the Negroes as laborers. "Not one of these colonies ever was or ever can be brought to any considerable improvement without a supply of white servants and Negroes," declared the Council of Montserrat in 1680. In a European society in which subordination was considered essential, in which [Edmund] Burke could speak of the working classes as "miserable sheep" and Voltaire as "canaille." . . . —in such a society it is unnecessary to seek for apologies for the condition of the white servant in the colonies.

[Daniel] Defoe bluntly stated that the white servant was a slave. He was not. The servants' loss of liberty was of limited duration, the Negro was slave for life. The servant's status could not descend to his offspring, Negro children took the status of the mother. The master at no time had absolute control over the person and liberty of his servant as he had over his slave. The servant had rights, limited but recognized by law and inserted in a contract. He enjoyed, for instance, a limited right to property. In actual law the conception of the servant as a piece of property never went beyond that of personal estate and never reached the stage of a chattel or real estate. The laws in the colonies maintained this rigid distinction and visited cohabitation between the races with severe penalties. The servant could aspire, at the end of his term, to a plot of land, though . . . it was not a legal right, and conditions varied from colony to colony. The serf in Europe could therefore hope for an early freedom in America which villeinage could not afford. The freed servants became small yeoman farmers, settled in the back country, a democratic force in a society of large aristocratic plantation owners, and were the pioneers in westward expansion. . . .

The institution of white servitude, however, had grave disadvantages [Malachy] Postlethwayt, a rigid mercantilist, argued that white laborers in the colonies would tend to create rivalry with the mother country in manufacturing. Better black slaves on plantations than white servants in industry, which would encourage aspirations to independence. The supply moreover was becoming increasingly difficult, and the need of the plantations outstripped the English convictions. In addition, merchants were involved in many vexatious and costly proceedings arising from people signifying their willingness to emigrate, accepting food and clothes in advance, and then sueing for unlawful detention. Indentured servants were not forthcoming in sufficient quantities to replace those who had served their term. On the plantations, escape was easy for the white servant; less easy for the Negro who, if freed, tended, in self-defense, to stay in his locality where he was well known and less likely to be apprehended as a vagrant or runaway slave. The servant expected land at the end of his contract; the Negro, in a strange environment, conspicuous by his color and features, and ignorant of the white man's language and ways, could be kept permanently divorced from the land. Racial differences made it easier to justify and rationalize Negro slavery, to exact the mechanical obedience of a plough-ox or a cart-horse, to demand that resignation and that complete moral and intellectual subjection which alone make slave labor possible. Finally, and this was the decisive factor, the Negro slave was cheaper. The money which procured a white man's services for ten years could buy a Negro for life. As the governor of Barbados stated, the Barbadian planters found by experience that "three blacks work better and cheaper than one white man."

But the experience with white servitude had been invaluable. Kidnaping in Africa encountered no such difficulties as were encountered in England. Captains and ships had the experience of the one trade to guide them in the other. Bristol, the center of the servant trade, became one of the centers of the slave trade. Capital accumulated from the one financed the other. White servitude was the historic base upon which Negro slavery was constructed. The felon-drivers in the plantations became without effort slave-drivers. "In significant numbers," writes Professor [U. B.] Phillips, "the Africans were latecomers fitted into a system already developed."

Here, then, is the origin of Negro slavery. The reason was economic, not racial; it had to do not with the color of the laborer, but the cheapness of the labor. As compared with Indian and white labor, Negro slavery was eminently superior. . . . The features of the man, his hair, color and dentifrice, his "sub-human" characteristics so widely pleaded, were only the later rationalizations to justify a simple economic fact: that the colonies needed labor and resorted to Negro labor because it was cheapest and best. This was not a theory, it was a practical conclusion deduced from the personal experience of the planter. He would have gone to the moon, if necessary, for labor. Africa was nearer than the moon, nearer too than the more populous countries of India and China. But their turn was to come.

This white servitude is of cardinal importance for an understanding of the development of the New World and the Negro's place in that development. It completely explodes the old myth that the whites could not stand the strain of manual labor in the climate of the New World and that, for this reason and this reason alone, the European powers had recourse to Africans. The argument is quite untenable. A Mississippi dictum will have it that "only black men and mules can face the sun in July." But the whites faced the sun for well over a hundred years in Barbados, and the Salzburgers of Georgia indignantly denied that rice cultivation was harmful to them. The Caribbean islands are well within the tropical zone, but their climate is more equable than tropical, the temperature rarely exceeds 80 degrees though it remains uniform the whole year round, and they are exposed to the gentle winds from the sea. The unbearable humidity of an

August day in some parts of the United States has no equal in the islands. Moreover only the southern tip of Florida in the United States is actually tropical, yet Negro labor flourished in Virginia and Carolina. The southern parts of the United States are not hotter than South Italy or Spain, and de Tocqueville asked why the European could not work there as well as in those two countries? When [Eli] Whitney invented his cotton gin, it was confidently expected that cotton would be produced by free labor on small farms, and it was, in fact, so produced. Where the white farmer was ousted, the enemy was not the climate but the slave plantation, and the white farmer moved westward, until the expanding plantation sent him on his wanderings again. . . . In our own time we who have witnessed the dispossession of Negroes by white sharecroppers in the South and the mass migration of Negroes from the South to the colder climates of Detroit, New York, Pittsburgh and other industrial centers of the North, can no longer accept the convenient rationalization that Negro labor was employed on the slave plantations because the climate was too rigorous for the constitution of the white man. . . .

Where the whites disappeared, the cause was not the climate but the supersession of the small farm by the large plantation, with its consequent demand for a large and steady supply of labor.

The climatic theory of the plantation is thus nothing but a rationalization. In an excellent essay on the subject Professor Edgar Thompson writes: "The plantation is not to be accounted for by climate. It is a political institution." It is, we might add, more: it is an economic institution. . . .

The history of Australia clinches the argument. Nearly half of this island continent lies within the tropical zone. In part of this tropical area, the state of Queensland, the chief crop is sugar. When the industry began to develop, Australia had a choice of two alternatives: black labor or white labor. The commonwealth began its sugar cultivation in the usual way—with imported black labor from the Pacific islands. Increasing demands, however, were made for a white Australia policy, and in the twentieth century non-white immigration was prohibited. It is irrelevant to consider here that as a result the cost of production of Australian sugar is prohibitive, that the industry is artificial and survives only behind the Chinese wall of Australian autarchy. Australia was willing to pay a high price in order to remain a white man's country. Our sole concern here with the question is that this price was paid from the pockets of the Australian consumer and not in the physical degeneration of the Australian worker. . . .

Negro slavery, thus, had nothing to do with climate. Its origin can be expressed in three words: in the Caribbean, Sugar; on the mainland, Tobacco and Cotton. A change in the economic structure produced a corresponding change in the labor supply. . . . Sugar, tobacco, and cotton required the large plantation and hordes of cheap labor, and the small farm of the ex-indentured white servant could not possibly survive. The tobacco of the small farm in Barbados was displaced by the sugar of the large plantation. The rise of the sugar industry in the Caribbean was the signal for a gigantic dispossession of the small farmer. Barbados in 1645 had 11,200 small white farmers and 5,680 Negro slaves; in 1667 there were 745 large plantation owners and 82,023 slaves. In 1645 the island had 18,300 whites fit to bear arms, in 1667 only 8,300. The white farmers were squeezed out. . . .

Where the plantation did not develop, as in the Cuban tobacco industry, Negro labor was rare and white labor predominated. The liberal section of the Cuban population consistently advocated the cessation of the Negro slave trade and the introduction of white immigrants. [José Antonio] Saco, mouthpiece of the liberals, called for the immigration of workers "white and free, from all parts of the world, of all races, provided they have a white face and can do honest labor." Sugar defeated Saco. It was the sugar plantation, with its servile base, which retarded white immigration in nineteenth century Cuba as it had banned it in seventeenth century Barbados and eighteenth century Saint Domingue. No sugar, no Negroes. In Puerto Rico, which developed relatively late as a genuine plantation, and where, before the American regime, sugar never dominated the lives and thoughts of the population as it did elsewhere, the poor white peasants survived and the Negro slaves never exceeded fourteen per cent of the population. Saco wanted to "whiten" the Cuban social structure. Negro slavery blackened that structure all over the Caribbean while the blood of the Negro slaves reddened the Atlantic and both its shores. Strange that an article like sugar, so sweet and necessary to human existence, should have occasioned such crimes and bloodshed! . . .

4

# THE SOUTHERN LABOR SYSTEM

Oscar Handlin and his wife, Mary Flug Handlin, are a remarkable team of American historians who have cast their nets widely over many aspects of social history. A leading authority on immigration, Handlin (1915- ) —the Charles Warren Professor of American History at Harvard University—comes to the question of the Negro in the New World from a different perspective than most researchers. The Negro is not simply another immigrant group, of course, for he came unwillingly, but originally he did come with another body of new arrivals, the indentured servant. In the essay that follows the Handlins explore the ways in which the status of servant and slave came to be separated.

In the bitter years before the Civil War, and after, men often turned to history for an explanation of the disastrous difference that divided the nation against itself. It seemed as if some fundamental fault must account for the tragedy that was impending or that had been realized; and it was tempting then to ascribe the troubles of the times to an original separateness between the sections that fought each other in 1861.

The last quarter century has banished from serious historical thinking the ancestral cavaliers and roundheads with whom the rebels and Yankees had peopled their past. But there is still an inclination to accept as present from the start a marked divergence in the character of the labor force, free whites in the North, Negro slaves in the South. Most commonly, the sources of that divergence are discovered in geography. In the temperate North, it is held, English ways were transposed intact. But the soil and climate of the South favored the production of staples, most efficiently raised under a regime of plantation slavery.

In this case, however, it is hardly proper to load nature with responsibility for human institutions. Tropical crops and climate persisted in the South after 1865 when its labor system changed, and they were there before it appeared. Negro slavery was not spontaneously produced by heat, humidity, and tobacco. An examination of the condition and status of seventeenth-century labor will show that slavery was not there from the start, that it was not simply imitated from elsewhere, and that it was not a response to any unique qualities in the Negro himself. It emerged rather from the adjustment to American conditions of traditional European institution.

By the latter half of the eighteenth century, slavery was a clearly defined status. It was

> that condition of a natural person, in which, by the operation of law, the application of his physical and mental powers depends . . . upon the will of another . . . and in which he is incapable . . . of . . . holding property [or any other rights] . . . except as the agent or instrument of another. In slavery, . . . the state, in ignoring the personality of the slave, . . . commits the control of his conduct . . . to the master, together with the power of transferring his authority to another.[1]

Thinking of slavery in that sense, the Englishmen of 1772 could boast with Lord Mansfield that their country had never tolerated the institution; simply to touch the soil of England made men free.[2] But the distinction between slave and free that had become important by the eighteenth century was not a significant distinction at the opening of the seventeenth century. In the earlier period, the antithesis of "free" was not "slave" but unfree; and, within the condition of unfreedom, law and practice recognized several gradations.

The status that involved the most complete lack of freedom was villeinage, a servile condition transmitted from father to son. The villein was limited in the right to hold property or make contracts; he could be bought and sold with the land he worked or without, and had "to do all that that the Lord will him command"; while the lord could "rob, beat, and chastise his Villain at his will." It was true that the condition had almost ceased to exist in England itself. But it persisted in Scotland well into the eighteenth century. . . .

Early modification in the laws regulating servitude did not, in England or the colonies, alter essentially the nature of the condition. Whether voluntary or involuntary, the status did not involve substantially more freedom in law than villeinage. It was not heritable; but servants could be bartered for a profit, sold to the highest bidder for the unpaid debts of their masters, and otherwise transferred like movable goods or chattels. Their capacity to hold property was narrowly limited as was their right to make contracts. Furthermore, the master had extensive powers of discipline, enforced by physical chastisement or by extension of the term of service. Offenses against the state also brought on punishments different from those meted out to free men; with no property to be fined, the servants were whipped. In every civic, social, and legal attribute, these victims of the turbulent displacements of the sixteenth and seventeenth centuries were set apart. Despised by every other order, without apparent means of rising to a more favored place, these men, and their children, and their children's children seemed mired in a hard, degraded life. That they formed a numerous element in society was nothing to lighten their lot.

The condition of the first Negroes in the continental English colonies must be viewed within the perspective of these conceptions and realities of servitude. As Europeans penetrated the dark continent in search of gold and ivory, they developed incidentally the international trade in Blacks. The Dutch in particular found this an attractive means of breaking into the business of the Spanish colonies, estopped by the policy of their own government from adding freely to their supply of African labor. In the course of this exchange through the West Indies, especially through Curacao, occasional small lots were left along the coast between Virginia and Massachusetts.

Through the first three-quarters of the seventeenth century, the Negroes, even in the South, were not numerous; nor were they particularly concentrated in any district. They came into a society in which a large part of the population was to some degree unfree; indeed in Virginia under the Company almost everyone, even tenants and laborers, bore some sort of servile obligation. The Negroes' lack of freedom was not unusual. These newcomers, like so many others, were accepted, bought and held, as kinds of servants. They were certainly not well off. But their ill-fortune was of a sort they shared with men from England, Scotland, and Ireland, and with the unlucky aborigenes held in captivity. Like the others, some Negroes became free, that is, terminated their period of service. Some became artisans; a few became landowners and the masters of other men. The status of Negroes was that of servants; and so they were identified and treated down to the 1660's.

The word, "slave" was, of course, used occasionally. It had no meaning in English law, but there was a significant colloquial usage. This was a general term of derogation. It served to express contempt; "O what a rogue and peasant slave am I," says Hamlet (Act II, Scene 2). It also described the low-born as contrasted with the gentry; of two hundred warriors, a sixteenth-century report said, eight were gentlemen, the rest slaves. The implication of degradation was also transferred to the low kinds of labor; "In this hal," wrote [Thomas] More (1551), "all vyle seruice, all slauerie . . . is done by bondemen."

It was in this sense that Negro servants were sometimes called slaves. But the same appellation was, in England, given to other non-English servants,—to a Russian, for instance. In Europe and in the American colonies, the term was, at various times and places, applied indiscriminately to Indians, mulattoes, and mestizos, as well as to Negroes. For that matter, it applied also to white Englishmen. It thus commonly described the servitude of children; so, the poor planters complained, "Our children, the parents dieinge" are held as "slaues or drudges" for the discharge of their parents' debts. Penal servitude too was often referred to as slavery; and the phrase, "slavish servant" turns up from time to time. Slavery had no meaning in law; at most it was a popular description of a low form of service.

Yet in not much more than a half century after 1660 this term of derogation was transformed into a fixed legal position. In a society characterized by many degrees of unfreedom, the Negro fell into a status novel to English law, into an unknown condition toward which the colonists unsteadily moved, slavery in its eighteenth- and nineteenth-century form. The available accounts do not explain this development because they assume that this form of slavery was known from the start. . . .

If chattel slavery was not present from the start, nor adopted from elsewhere, it was also not a response to any inherent qualities that fitted the Negro for plantation labor. There has been a good deal of speculation as to the relative efficiency of free and slave, of Negro, white, and Indian, labor. Of necessity, estimates of which costs were higher, which risks—through mortality, escape, and rebellion—greater, are inconclusive. What is conclusive is the fact that Virginia and Maryland planters did not think Negro labor more desirable. A preference for white servants persisted even on the islands. But when the Barbadians could not get those, repeated representations in London made known their desire for Negroes. No such demands came from the continental colonies. On the contrary the calls are for skilled white labor with the preference for those most like the first settlers and ranging down from Scots and Welsh to Irish, French, and Italians. Least desired were the unskilled, utterly strange Negroes.

It is quite clear in fact that as late as 1669 those who thought of large-scale agriculture assumed it would be manned not by Negroes but by white peasants under a condition of villeinage. John Locke's constitutions for South Carolina envisaged an hereditary group of servile "leetmen"; and Lord Shaftsbury's signory on Locke Island in 1674 actually attempted to put that scheme into practice. If the holders of large estates in the Chesapeake colonies expressed no wish for a Negro labor supply, they could hardly have planned to use black hands as a means of displacing white, whether as a concerted plot by restoration courtiers to set up a new social order in America, or as a program for lowering costs.

Yet the Negroes did cease to be servants and became slaves, ceased to be men in whom masters held a proprietary interest and became chattels, objects that were the property of their owners. In that transformation originated the southern labor system.

Although the colonists assumed at the start that all servants would "fare alike in the colony," the social realities of their situation early gave rise to differences of treatment. It is not necessary to resort to racialist assumptions to account for such measures; these were simply the reactions of immigrants lost to the stability and security of home and isolated in an immense wilderness in which threats from the unknown were all about them. Like the millions who would follow, these immigrants longed in the strangeness for the company of familiar men and singled out to be welcomed those who were most like themselves. So the measures regulating settlement spoke specifically in this period of differential treatment for various groups. From time to time, regulations applied only to "those of our own nation," or to the French, the Dutch, the Italians, the Swiss, the Palatines, the Welsh, the Irish, or to combinations of the diverse nationalities drawn to these shores.

In the same way the colonists became aware of the differences between themselves and the African immigrants. The rudeness of the Negroes' manners, the strangeness of their languages, the difficulty of communicating to them English notions of morality and proper behavior occasioned sporadic laws to regulate their conduct. So, Bermuda's law to restrain the insolencies of Negroes "who are servents" (that is, their inclination to run off with the pigs of others) was the same in kind as the legislation that the Irish should "straggle not night or dai, as is too common with them." Until the 1660's the statutes on the Negroes were not at all unique. Nor did they add up to a decided trend.

But in the decade after 1660 far more significant differentiations with regard to term of service, relationship to Christianity, and disposal of children, cut the Negro apart from all other servants and gave a new depth to his bondage.

In the early part of the century duration of service was of only slight importance. Certainly in England where labor was more plentiful than the demand, expiration of a term had little meaning; the servant was free only to enter upon another term, while the master had always the choice of taking on the old or a new servitor. That situation obtained even in America as long as starvation was a real possibility. In 1621, it was noted, "vittles being scarce in the country noe man wil tacke servants." As late as 1643 Lord Baltimore thought it better if possible to hire labor than to risk the burden of supporting servants through a long period. Under such conditions the number of years specified in the indenture was not important, and if a servant had no indenture the question was certainly not likely to rise.

That accounts for the early references to unlimited service. Thus Sandys's plan for Virginia in 1618 spoke of tenants-at-half assigned to the treasurer's office, to "belong to said office for ever." Again, those at Berkeley's Hundred were perpetual "after the manner of estates in England." Since perpetual in seventeenth-century law meant that which had "not any set time expressly allotted for [its] . . . continuance," such provisions were not surprising. Nor was it surprising to find instances in the court records of Negroes who seemed to serve forever. These were quite compatible with the possibility of ultimate freedom. Thus a colored man bought in 1644 "as a Slave for Ever," nevertheless was held "to serve as other Christians servants do" and freed after a term.

The question of length of service became critical when the mounting value of labor eased the fear that servants would be a drain on "vittles" and raised the expectation of profit from their toil. Those eager to multiply the number of available hands by stimulating immigration had not only to overcome the reluctance of a prospective newcomer faced with the trials of a sea journey; they had also to counteract the widespread reports in England and Scotland that servants were harshly treated and bound in perpetual slavery.

To encourage immigration therefore, the colonies embarked upon a line of legislation designed to improve servants' conditions and to enlarge the prospect of a meaningful release, a release that was not the start of a new period of servitude, but of life as a freeman and landowner. Thus Virginia, in 1642, discharged "publick tenants from their servitudes, who, like one sort of villians anciently in England" were attached to the lands of the governor; and later laws provided that no person was to "be adjudged to serve the collonie hereafter." Most significant were the statutes which reassured prospective newcomers by setting limits to the terms of servants without indentures, in 1638/9 in Maryland, in 1642/3 in Virginia. These acts seem to have applied only to voluntary immigrants "of our own nation." The Irish and other aliens, less desirable, at first received longer terms. But the realization that such discrimination retarded "the peopling of the country" led to an extension of the identical privilege to all Christians.

But the Negro never profited from these enactments. Farthest removed from the English, least desired, he communicated with no friends who might be deterred from following. Since his coming was involuntary, nothing that happened to him would increase or decrease his numbers. To raise the status of Europeans by shortening their terms would ultimately increase the available hands by inducing their compatriots to emigrate; to reduce the Negro's term would produce an immediate loss and no ultimate gain. By mid-century the servitude of Negroes seems generally lengthier than that of whites; and thereafter the consciousness dawns that the Blacks will toil for the whole of their lives, not through any particular concern with their status but simply by contrast with those whose years of labor are limited by statute. The legal position of the Negro is, however, still uncertain; it takes legislative action to settle that.

The Maryland House, complaining of that ambiguity, provoked the decisive measure; "All Negroes and other slaves," it was enacted, "shall serve Durante Vita." Virginia reached the same end more tortuously. An act of 1661 had assumed, in imposing penalties on runaways, that *some* Negroes served for life. The law of 1670 went further; "all servants not being christians" brought in by sea were declared slaves for life.

But slavery for life was still tenuous as long as the slave could extricate himself by baptism. The fact that Negroes were heathens had formerly justified their bondage, since infidels were "perpetual" enemies of Christians. It had followed that conversion was a way to freedom. Governor [John] Archdale thus released the Spanish Indians captured to be sold as slaves to Jamaica when he learned they were Christians. As labor rose in value this presumption dissipated the zeal of masters for proselytizing. So that they be "freed from this doubt" a series of laws between 1667 and 1671 laid down the rule that conversion alone did not lead to a release from servitude. Thereafter manumission, which other servants could demand by right at the end of their terms, in the case of Negroes lay entirely within the discretion of the master.

A difference in the status of the offspring of Negro and white servants followed inevitably from the differentiation in the length of their terms. The problem of disposing of the issue of servants was at first general. Bastardy, prevalent to begin with and more frequent as the century advanced, deprived the master of his women's work and subjected him to the risk of their death. Furthermore the parish was burdened with the support of the child. The usual procedure was to punish the offenders with fines or whippings and to compel the servant to serve beyond his time for the benefit of the parish and to recompense the injured master.

The general rule ceased to apply once the Negro was bound for life, for there was no means of extending his servitude. The most the outraged master could get was the child, a minimal measure of justice, somewhat tempered by the trouble of rearing the infant to an age of usefulness. The truly vexing problem was to decide on the proper course when one parent was free, for it was not certain whether the English law that the issue followed the state of the father would apply. Maryland, which adopted that rule in 1664, found that unscrupulous masters instigated intercourse between their Negro males and white females which not only gave them the offspring, but, to boot, the service of the woman for the life of her husband. The solution in Virginia which followed the precedent of the bastardy laws and had the issue follow the mother seemed preferable and ultimately was adopted in Maryland and elsewhere.

By the last quarter of the seventeenth century, one could distinguish clearly between the Negro slave who served for life and the servant for a period. But there was not yet a demarcation in personal terms: the servant was not yet a free man, nor the slave a chattel. As late as 1686, the words slave and servant could still be conflated to an extent that indicated men conceived of them as extensions of the same condition. . . .

It was the persistence of such conceptions that raised the fear that "noe free borne Christians will ever be induced to come over servants" without overwhelming assurance that there would be nothing slavish in their lot. After all Pennsylvania and New York now gave the European newcomer a choice of destination. In Virginia and Maryland there was a persistent effort to make immigration more attractive by further ameliorating the lot of European servants. The custom of the country undoubtedly moved more rapidly than the letter of the law. "Weake and Ignorant" juries on which former servants sat often decided cases against masters. But even the letter of the law showed a noticeable decline in the use of the death penalty and in the power of masters over men. By 1705 in some colonies, white servants were no longer transferable; they could not be whipped without a court order; and they were protected against the avaricious unreasonable masters who attempted to force them into new contracts "some small tyme before the expiration of their tyme of service."

Meanwhile the condition of the Negro deteriorated. In these very years, a startling growth in numbers complicated the problem. The Royal African Company was, to some extent, responsible, though its operations in the mainland colonies formed only a very minor part of its business. But the opening of Africa to free trade in 1698 inundated Virginia, Maryland, and South Carolina with new slaves. Under the pressure of policing these newcomers the regulation of Negroes actually grew harsher.

The early laws against runaways, against drunkenness, against carrying arms or trading without permission had applied penalties as heavy as death to all servants, Negroes and whites. But these regulations grew steadily less stringent in the case of white servants. On the other hand fear of the growing number of slaves, uneasy suspicion of plots and conspiracies, led to more stringent control of Negroes and a broad view of the master's power of discipline. Furthermore the emerging difference in treatment was calculated to create a real division of interest between Negroes on the one hand and whites on the other. Servants who ran away in the company of slaves, for instance, were doubly punished, for the loss of their own time and for the time of the slaves, a provision that discouraged such joint ventures. Similarly Negroes, even when freed, retained some disciplinary links with their less fortunate fellows. The wardens continued to supervise their children, they were not capable of holding white servants, and serious restrictions limited the number of manumissions.

The growth of the Negro population also heightened the old concern over sexual immorality and the conditions of marriage. The law had always recognized the interest of the lord in the marriage of his villein or neife and had frowned on the mixed marriage of free and unfree. Similarly it was inclined to hold that the marriage of any servant was a loss to the master, an "Enormous offense" productive of much detriment "against the law of God," and therefore dependent on the consent of the master. Mixed marriages of free men and servants were particularly frowned upon as complicating status and therefore limited by law.

There was no departure from these principles in the early cases of Negro-white relationships. Even the complicated laws of Maryland in 1664 and the manner of their enactment revealed no change in attitude. The marriage of Blacks and whites was possible; what was important was the status of the partners and their issue. It was to guard against the complications of status that the laws after 1691 forbade "spurious" or illegitimate mixed marriages of the slave and the free and punished violations with heavy penalties. Yet it was also significant that by then the prohibition was couched in terms, not simply of slave and free man, but of Negro and white. Here was evidence as in the policing regulations of an emerging demarkation.

The first settlers in Virginia had been concerned with the

difficulty of preserving the solidarity of the group under the disruptive effects of migration. They had been enjoined to "keepe to themselves" not to "marry nor give in marriage to the heathen, that are uncircumcised." But such resolutions were difficult to maintain and had gradually relaxed until the colonists included among "themselves" such groups as the Irish, once the objects of very general contempt. A common lot drew them together; and it was the absence of a common lot that drew these apart from the Negro. At the opening of the eighteenth century, the Black was not only set off by economic and legal status; he was "abominable," another order of man. . . .

Color then emerged as the token of the slave status; the trace of color became the trace of slavery. It had not always been so; as late as the 1660's the law had not even a word to describe the children of mixed marriages. But two decades later, the term mulatto is used, and it serves, not as in Brazil, to whiten the Black, but to affiliate through the color tie the offspring of a spurious union with his inherited slavery. (The compiler of the Virginia laws then takes the liberty of altering the texts to bring earlier legislation into line with his own new notions.) Ultimately the complete judicial doctrine begins to show forth, a slave cannot be a white man, and every man of color was descendent of a slave.

The rising wall dividing the legal status of the slave from that of the servant was buttressed by other developments which derogated the qualities of the Negro as a human being to establish his inferiority and thus completed his separation from the white. The destruction of the black man's personality involved, for example, a peculiar style of designation. In the seventeenth century many immigrants in addition to the Africans—Swedes, Armenians, Jews—had brought no family names to America. By the eighteenth all but the Negroes had acquired them. In the seventeenth century, Indians and Negroes bore names that were either an approximation of their original ones or similar to those of their masters,—Diana, Jane, Frank, Juno, Anne, Maria, Jenny. In the eighteenth century slaves seem increasingly to receive classical or biblical appellations, by analogy with Roman and Hebrew bondsmen. Deprivation by statute and usage of other civic rights, to vote, to testify, to bring suit, even if free, completed the process. And after 1700 appear the full slave codes, formal recognition that the Negroes are not governed by the laws of other men. . . .

## NOTES

1. Summarized in John Codman Hurd, *Law of Freedom and Bondage in the United States* (Boston, 1858), I, 42-43.
2. See Jerome Nadelhaft, "The Somersett Case and Slavery: Myth, Reality, and Repercussions," *The Journal of Negro History*, LI ( July, 1966), 193-208. (Editor's note.)

5

# DEBT-BONDAGE IN MALAYA

Forms of debt-bondage have been quite common. Not slavery, not indenture, debt-bondage lay in a legal and moral gray area, and relatively little is known about it. In 1958 an English member of the Malayan Civil Service, John M. Gullick (1916-     ), both anthropologist and historian, provided the first coherent description of how the system worked within the sultanates of the Malay peninsula. Debt-bondage, as will be seen, reached into the present century. As this selection makes clear, any examination of the practice of slavery must extend into other forms of involuntary, but non-penal, bondage, for Western scholars have too long been inclined to limit their investigations to those areas of Africa and the New World from which the more persistent and massive forms of slavery have arisen. In a later selection, in Part IV, we will return to the question of slavery by other names.

Debt-bondage was a useful means of recruitment of followers since debtors, unlike mercenaries and free volunteers, could not desert their master at will. A debt-bondsman was *orang berhutang* and a slave was *abdi* or *hamba*.

The European administrators who went into the Malay States

in 1874 wrote many reports on "debt-slavery." Slavery (in which they included debt-bondage) was a subject on which they and public opinion in the United Kingdom held strong views. The reports were thus written with a prejudice towards the subject-matter. The writers of the reports tended to generalize and to state as facts the stories told them by runaway bondsmen who had taken refuge with them and who had an interest in exaggerating their wrongs. Reports based on such data are not likely to be balanced and reliable. On the other hand after the revolt of 1875 known as the Perak War there was a more cautious and objective attitude to the subject since mishandling of the "debt-bondage" question had been one of the causes of that revolt.

The best general account of debt-bondage is given by [Frank] Swettenham [a British administrator]. After explaining that chiefs did not permit their subjects to accumulate wealth he goes on:

> Thus when a *rayat* (or subject) is in want of money he goes to his *Raja* or chief to lend it him, because he alone can do so. Either money or goods are then lent, and a certain time stipulated for payment. If at the expiry of that time the money is not paid, it is usual to wait some time longer, say two or three or even six months. Should payment not then be made, the debtor, if a single man, is taken into the creditor's house; he becomes one of his followers and is bound to execute any order and do any work the Raja as creditor may demand, until the debt is paid, however long a time that may be. During this time the Raja usually provides the debtor with food and clothing, but if the creditor gives him money, that money is added to the debt. Often, however, the Raja gives nothing and the debtor has to find food and clothing as he can. Should the debtor marry—and the Raja will in all probability find him a wife—the wife and descendants are equally in debt bondage.
>
> If, however, a large family were in bondage for the debt, one whose numbers seeemd to the Raja to add to

> his dignity, then he would probably refuse to accept payment, not absolutely, but would say Wait, and the waiting might last for years.

The debtor's work and services did not count towards reduction of the debt. Moreover the right of redemption was only nominal.

It is clear from this passage that debt-bondage, although in form an economic institution, was in substance a very mixed complex of several elements. The chief acquired and retained bondsmen as a means of augmenting his power and prestige. The bondsman might expect the creditor to provide him with a wife; the children of this union inherited the debtor status of the parent. The debtor's services, although considered to have some economic value, did not count towards the reduction of the debt. The debtor was usually a dependent of the creditor. Single men became followers, but not married men.

Debt-bondage was particularly significant in terms of the social relationship between the parties. This fact appears particularly in the information given about the transfer of debtors during the period of British protection. The rule was that a debtor could demand to be transferred to any other creditor who would pay off his debt to the original creditor. In practice transfers at the instance of the debtor were rare. Transfers at the instance of the creditor were common. . . . Transfer broke the personal tie which had grown out of the economic relationship. . . . [Governor] Hugh Clifford noted that:

> There is no special hardship in this (bondage) as the children grow up as dependents on the sons of the house and are fed and clothed, and as a rule are kindly treated by their masters.

. . . This idyllic picture is not to be accepted without reservation. The early reports contain instances of ill-treatment of debtors supported by the personal knowledge of the reporting officer.

When one human being is at the mercy of another, there will always be abuses of power. The question is not whether there were ever cases of ill-treatment but whether such cases were typical. . . . On balance it seems fair to conclude that the ruling class treated their bondsmen and slaves fairly. The vice of the system was that the bondsmen and slaves were inferior beings, almost chattels.

The economic aspect of debt-bondage, although it was not perhaps the most significant facet of the institution, deserves consideration. Here a distinction must be made between bondsmen who were and those who were not members of the household and personal following of the creditor.

Debt-bondsmen who were followers of their creditor were indeed an investment which could be realized by sale. They were thus of economic value as capital. But from the standpoint of income and expenditure they cost more to keep than their services were worth. The nature of their relationship with the creditor as "hangers on" precluded the possibility of their being given regular employment. If they had been assigned tasks, they would not have been available at beck and call. Long periods of idleness inevitably beget demoralization. . . . Swettenham noted that among debt-bondsmen "gambling becomes a mania" and elsewhere relates how on leaving an aristocratic household one morning he could not get anyone to carry his baggage down to the boat because "all Che Mida's people were overcome by the effect of opium smoked the night bfore."

The question of the economic value of followers who were debtors came to a head when British administrators suggested that debt-bondage should be gradually abolished by counting the presumed value of the debtors' serviecs against their debts. Malay chiefs in Perak replied that the services of their bondsmen had a value "which was scarcely more than nominal."

Debt-bondsmen not in the personal following of their creditors were generally married men with families. They were put to agricultural work to produce food for the sustenance of their creditor and his household. They thus contributed to providing the surplus with which to maintain a section of the community in a non-productive military and political role.

The most detailed account of the work of agricultural debt-bondsmen relates to Kedah when it came under British protection in 1909. There were three types of work—(1) *kerja panjang pendek*, odd jobs of personal and domestic service; (2) *kerja dalam bendang*, cultivation in the rice fields; and (3) *kerja dalam dusun*, care of orchards. This last type of work was regarded as nominal and did not entitle the debtor to receive food and clothing from the creditor. Of Perak in the 1870's it was said that the work of a bondsman was "every species of household drudgery, in clearing ground, and in raising padi and other articles of food. Another observer said of a chief's bondsmen in Perak that "they served in his household, cultivated his fields and worked his mines."

The services of an agricultural bondsman relieved a chief of the necessity of cultivating the food which he ate and of doing domestic chores of one kind and another. He thus had leisure for military and political pursuits. There was no attempt, with the exception of some small ventures in tin-mining, to organize bondsmen for production on a large or industrial scale so as to obtain a surplus for sale. The explanation of this fact lies in the absence of market outlets for large quantities of produce and the lack of managerial staff for the organization of large-scale enterprises of this kind.

The assignment of agricultural labour to people of low status had the inevitable consequence that no one of aristocratic birth would willingly demean himself to do such work.

A chief's following included a number of women who were for the most part either bondswomen or slaves. Some had been purchased or born into bondage. Others had been rounded up from the villages of the district under the custom which permitted a chief to recruit women as concubines or domestic servants in this way. To judge from the records this class of people in bondage had more cause for complaint than any other. . . . There is some doubt as to the extent to which prostitution was voluntary or was forced upon them. It was clearly of common occurrence except among the women reserved as concubines of the creditor.

This female retinue was kept as the means of satisfying the sexual appetites of the young, unmarried men who formed the chief's armed following. A chief thus gained two objects. He had the means of attracting to him men in search of mistresses and ultimately of wives. Secondly by providing his followers with the means of satisfying their sexual needs at home the chief prevented them from making forays among his peasant subjects to seduce or abduct their women. No doubt the chief had first to abduct some of these women himself under a more or less legal procedure. But this method was to be preferred to allowing his followers to make raids of their own. If they had done so, the chief's peasant subjects would either have fought back or more probably would have fled. In either case the chief would have been the poorer.

It was a recognized custom that a follower might ask his chief to give him a wife from among the women in his household. There is also evidence that a Sultan, and possibly a district chief, had a right of control over the marriages of all women in the village in which he lived.

A female follower who became a concubine of her master and bore him a child was said to be entitled to her freedom. She must at least have achieved higher status in bondage in that way.

Entry into debt-bondage was not always the unwelcome result of misfortune. It was observed that some voluntarily contracted debts when they knew well that it would lead to bondage.

If it is a fair conclusion that the average bondsman could look forward to reasonably good treatment and friendly relations with his creditor, it is surprising only that men would thus surrender their liberty and run the risk of encountering a bad master. The most likely explanation is that many followers of chiefs were men without a home. It was a period of migration and instability. A part of the population was mere flotsam and jetsam in a hostile world. In these circumstances a homeless man might be tempted to attach himself in bondage to a chief. He thus got a living, the protection of a powerful patron, access to women and the ultimate prospect of obtaining a wife. In this case, as in so many other relationships, the tie arose not so much from strength on one side and weakness on the other, as from mutual need. The follower needed a patron, a living and a wife. But the chief on his side needed a private army.

Much of what has been said of debt-bondsmen applies equally

to slaves. British administrators tended to classify the two groups together as "debt-slaves."

There were however certain differences. A slave was lower in status than a debt-bondsman who ranked as a free man (*orang merdeka*). A Malay observer states:

> While there was no difference in the nature of the work which the two classes of slaves were made to do for their masters, the debt slaves were less degrading (*sic*) than the ordinary slaves because the former were supposed to be able to redeem themselves by paying off their debts whereas the latter could not under any circumstances regain their freedom except by some act of grace on the part of their master.

The right of self-redemption was however only rarely exercised. The real distinction of status lay in the fact that debt-bondsmen (but not slaves) were still acknowledged as members of the same society as their masters. The distinction was rationalized by a rule which forbade the enslavement of Muslims by Muslims. Slaves therefore were mainly Africans, aborigines and Bataks (a non-Muslim Sumatran tribe).

There was a hierarchy of status even in bondage. A non-Muslim foreigner could be enslaved. A Muslim Malay peasant could not be enslaved but he could be reduced to debt-bondage. At the next higher level an impecunious aristocrat who became indebted to his patron was not usually treated as a debt-bondsman. Of the only such case which has been traced it was said by a son of the creditor that "a man like him is not expected to do menial work. He has opportunities of trading on his own account, and the only way his master requires his services is that he is obliged to attend on him." In effect an aristocrat could be a debtor but was not regarded as a debt-bondsman. It is an example of the pervasiveness of the status concept in the Malay social system.

*part two*

# *THE PROBLEM OF COMPARATIVE SLAVE SYSTEMS*

# 1

## NEW WORLD SYSTEMS

"Better to dispute the number of angels on a pinhead than to argue that one country's slavery is superior to another's." So responds an anthropologist, Marvin Harris, to comparative analyses of slave systems as conducted by those who attach value judgments to the relative harshness or benevolence of a system. But an awareness of differences need not lead to the conclusion—except if one wishes to be a propagandist for or against a culture—that these differences make one practice superior to another. Early in the present century historians began to be aware that there were fundamental differences between slave systems, not necessarily in the brutality by which they were transmitted to their subjects so much as in the legal definitions given to slavery itself. A student of the labor movement and of the Mexican revolution of 1910-11, Frank Tannenbaum (1893-1969), long a Professor of History at Columbia University, wrote the book which, from its publication in 1946, has been the chief target of historical revisionism and which attempted to show how and why systems did differ: *Slave and Citizen.* He placed particular emphasis on religious belief systems. Some detractors thought he was missing the moral point that evil has no dimensions: slavery, if bad, was evil whether extensive or limited, whether harsh or benign, for it was a denial of a fundamental human right to liberty. Tannenbaum recognized this, stating that slavery everywhere was always cruel by its nature, but he also thought that one could detect ways in which its force as perceived by its victims might be differentiated, as the following extract shows.

The Negro slave arriving in the Iberian Peninsula in the middle of the fifteenth century found a propitious environment. The setting, legal as well as moral, that made this easy transition possible was due to the fact that the people of the Iberian Peninsula were not strangers to slavery. . . .

Spanish law, custom, and tradition were transferred to America and came to govern the position of the Negro slave. It is interesting to note that a large body of new law was developed for the treatment of the Indians in America, whereas the Negro's position was covered by isolated *cedulas* dealing with special problems. It was not until 1789 that a formal code dealing with the Negro slave was promulgated. But this new code, as recognized by the preamble itself, is merely a summary of the ancient and traditional law. . . .

This body of law, containing the legal tradition of the Spanish people and also influenced by the Catholic doctrine of the equality of all men in the sight of God, was biased in favor of freedom and opened the gates to manumission when slavery was transferred to the New World. The law in Spanish and Portuguese America facilitated manumission, the tax-gatherer did not oppose it, and the church ranked it among the works singularly agreeable to God. A hundred social devices narrowed the gap between bondage and liberty, encouraged the master to release his slave, and the bondsman to achieve freedom on his own account. From the sixteenth to the nineteenth century, slaves in Brazil, by reimbursing the original purchase price, could compel their masters to free them. In Cuba and in Mexico the price might be fixed at the request of the Negro, and the slave was freed even if he cost "triple of the sum." The right to have his price declared aided the Negro in seeking a new master, and the owner was required to transfer him to another.

The law further permitted the slave to free himself by installments, and this became a widely spread custom, especially in Cuba. A slave worth six hundred dollars could buy himself out in twenty-four installments of twenty-five dollars each, and with every payment he acquired one twenty-fourth of his own freedom. Thus, when he had paid fifty dollars, he owned one twelfth of himself. On delivering his first installment, he could move from his master's house, and thereafter pay interest on the remaining sum, thus acquiring a position not materially different in effect from that of a man in debt who had specific monetary obligations. There seem to have been many instances of slaves paying out all of the installments due on their purchase price except the last fifty or one hundred dollars, and on these paying one half a real per day for every fifty pesos. The advantage in this arrangement apparently lay in the fact that a Negro, thus partially a slave, could escape the payment of taxes on his property and be free from military service.

In effect, slavery under both law and custom had, for all practical purposes, become a contractural arrangement between the master and his bondsman. There may have been no written contract between the two parties, but the state behaved, in ffect, as if such a contract did exist, and used its powers to enforce it. This presumed contract was of a strictly limited liability on the part of the slave, and the state, by employing the officially provided protector of slaves, could and did define the financial obligation of the slave to his master in each specific instance as it arose. Slavery had thus from a very early date, at least in so far as the practice was concerned, moved from a "status," or "caste," "by law of nature," or because of "innate inferiority," or because of the "just judgment and provision of holy script," to become a mere matter of an available sum of money for redemption. Slavery had become a matter of financial competence on the part of the slave, and by that fact lost a great part of the degrading imputation that attached to slavery where it was looked upon as evidence of moral or biological inferiority.

Slavery could be wiped out by a fixed purchase price, and therefore the taint of slavery proved neither very deep nor indelible.

In addition to making freedom something obtainable for money, which the slave had the right to acquire and possess, *the state made manumission possible for a number of other reasons.* A Negro could be freed if unduly punished by his master. He was at liberty to marry a free non-slave (and the master could not legally interfere), and as under the law the children followed the mother, a slave's children born of a free mother were also free. Slaves in Brazil who joined the army to fight in the Paraguayan war were freed by decree on November 6, 1866, and some twenty thousand Negroes were thus liberated.

In the wars of independence many thousands of slaves in Venezuela and Colombia were freed by Bolívar and enlisted in the army of liberation. In Argentina perhaps as many as a third of San Martín's host that crossed the Andes was composed of freed Negroes. And, finally, as early as 1733, by a special *cedula* repeated twice later, slaves escaping to Cuba from other West Indian islands because they wished to embrace the Catholic religion could be neither returned to their masters, nor sold, nor given in slavery to any other person.

But significant and varied as were these provisions of the law in the Spanish and Portuguese colonies, they were less important in the long run than the social arrangements and expectancies that prevailed. It was permissible for a slave child in Brazil to be freed at the baptismal font by an offer of twenty milreis, and in Cuba for twenty-five dollars. A female slave could seek a godfather for her baby in some respectable person, hoping that the moral obligation imposed upon the godfather would lead to freeing the child. It was both a meritorious and a pious deed to accept such a responsibility and to fulfill its implicit commitments, and it bestowed distinction upon him who accepted them. . . . A parent having ten children could claim freedom, whether male or female.

The freeing of one's slaves was an honorific tradition, and men fulfilled it on numerous occasions. Favorite wet nurses were often freed; slaves were manumitted on happy occasions in the family—a birth of a first son, or the marriage of one of the master's children. In fact, the excuses and the occasions were numerous—the passing of an examination in school by the young master, a family festival, a national holiday, and, of course, by will upon the death of the master. . . .

Opportunities for escape from slavery were further facilitated by the system of labor that prevailed in many places, particularly in cities. Slaves were often encouraged to hire themselves out and bring their masters a fixed part of their wages, keeping the rest. Skilled artisans, masons, carpenters, blacksmiths, wheelwrights, tailors, and musicians were special gainers from the arrangement. But even ordinary laborers were allowed to organize themselves in gangs, *gente de Ganho*, as they were called. Preceded by a leader, who would guide them in a rhythmic chant, they would offer their services as carriers on the wharves of the city or to do any heavy work that came to hand. . . .

With all its cruelty, abuse, hardship, and inhumanity, the atmosphere in Brazil and in the Spanish-American countries made for manumission. Even in the rural regions individuals were allowed to sell the products from their own plots, given them to work for themselves, and to save their money toward the day of freedom. In Cuba, one writer notes, the raising of pigs by slaves provided a ready source of the sums accumulated for such a purpose. It should be further noticed that, in addition to their Sundays, the Negroes in Brazil had many holidays, amounting all together to eighty-four days a year, which they could use for their own purposes, and for garnering such funds as their immediate skill and opportunities made possible. The purchase of one's freedom was so accepted a tradition among the Negroes that many a Negro bought the freedom of his wife and children while he himself continued laboring as a slave, and among the freed Negroes societies were organized for pooling resources and collecting funds for the freeing of their brethren still in bondage.

These many provisions favoring manumission were strongly influenced by the church. Without interfering with the institution of slavery where the domestic law accepted it, the church early condemned the slave trade and prohibited Catholics from taking part in it. The prohibition was not effective, though it in some measure may have influenced the Spaniards to a rather limited participation in the trade as such. The slave trade had been condemned by Pius II on October 7, 1462, by Paul III on May 29, 1537, by Urban VIII on April 2, 1639, by Benedict XIV on December 20, 1741, and finally by Gregory XVI on December 3, 1839. The grounds of the condemnation were that innocent and free persons were illegally and by force captured and sold into slavery, that rapine, cruelty, and war were stimulated in the search for human beings to be sold at a profit. The Franciscan Father Thomas Mercado had condemned the slave trade in the strongest terms in the year 1587, on the grounds that it fostered two thousand falsehoods, a thousand robberies, and a thousand deceptions. But the church did not interfere with the customary institution where it derived from known practices in a given community, such as born slaves, slaves taken in a just war, or those who had sold themselves or had been condemned by a legitimate court.

The presumption against the slave trade was that it forced people into slavery outside the law and against their will. More important in the long run than the condemnation of the slave trade proved the church's insistence that slave and master were equal in the sight of God. Whatever the formal relations between slave and master, they must both recognize their relationship to each other as moral human beings and as brothers in Christ. The master had an obligation to protect the spiritual integrity of the slave, to teach him the Christian religion, to help him achieve the privileges of the sacraments, to guide him into living a good life, and to protect him from mortal sin. The slave had a right to become a Christian, to be baptized, and to be considered a member of the Christian community. Baptism was considered his entrance into the community, and until he was sufficiently instructed to be able to receive it, he was looked upon as out of the community and as something less than human.

From the very beginning the Catholic churches in America insisted that masters bring their slaves to church to learn the doctrine and participate in the communion. The assembled bishops in Mexico in the year 1555 urged all Spaniards to send the Indians, and especially the Negroes, to church; similarly in Cuba in 1680. . . .

If the Latin-American environment was favorable to freedom,

the British and American were hostile.* Legal obstacles were placed in the way of manumission, and it was discouraged in every other manner. The presumption was in favor of slavery. A Negro who could not prove that he was free was presumed to be a runaway slave and was advertised as such; if no claimant appeared, he was sold at public auction for the public benefit. In Demerara no slave could be manumitted without the consent of the Governor and Council. In most of the British colonies heavy taxes had been imposed on manumission, and as late as 1802 a law was passed in the Northern Leeward Islands requiring the owner who would register his slave for manumission to pay five hundred pounds into the public treasury, and this sum had to be provided in his will if it made provision for the liberation of the slave. The slave could not be freed without the master's consent, even if the full price of the slave was offered. In the fear of an increase of freemen, Barbados, in 1801, passed a law taxing the manumission of a female slave much more heavily than a male. St. Christopher, which taxed manumission for the first time in 1802, declared it to be a "great inconvenience . . . that [the number of] free Negroes and . . . free persons of color was augmented" by releasing slaves

* There were, briefly speaking, three slave systems in the Western Hemisphere. The British, American, Dutch, and Danish were at one extreme, and the Spanish and Portuguese at the other. In between these two fell the French. The first of these groups is characterized by the fact that they had no effective slave tradition, no slave law, and that their religious institutions were little concerned about the Negro. At the other extreme there were both a slave law and a belief that the spiritual personality of the slave transcended his slave status. In between them the French suffered from the lack of a slave tradition and slave law, but did have the same religious principles as the Spaniards and Portuguese. If one were forced to arrange these systems of slavery in order of severity, the Dutch would seem to stand as the hardest, the Portuguese as the mildest, and the French, in between, as having elements of both.

from bondage, and provided that a slave who had been released by his master, but not formally enfranchised, should be "publicly sold at vendue."

In the southern part of the United States the position of the slave was closely similar to that in the British West Indies. What is important to note is the tendency to identify the Negro with the slave. The mere fact of being a Negro was presumptive of a slave status. South Carolina in 1740 (similarly Georgia and Mississippi) provided that "all negroes, Indians (those now free excepted) . . . mulattoes, or mestizos, who are or shall hereafter be in the province, and all their issue and offspring, born or to be born, shall be and they are hereby declared to be and remain forever hereafter absolute slaves and shall follow the condition of the mother." Equally striking is an early law of Maryland, dating from 1663: "All negroes or other slaves within the province, all negroes to be hereafter imported, shall serve *durante vita*"; and their children were to follow the condition of the father. Significantly the same law said: "That whatsoever freeborn women (English) shall intermarry with any slave . . . shall serve the master of such slave during the life of her husband; all the issue of such freeborn women, so married, shall be slave as their fathers were." A free Negro in South Carolina (1740) harboring a runaway slave, or charged "with any criminal matter," upon inability to pay the fine and court charges was to be sold "at public auction." The same state provided that an emancipated Negro set free otherwise than according to the act of 1800 could be seized and kept as a slave by "any person whatsoever."

The Negro was a slave, and the pressure seemed, in a number of states, anyway, to keep him one, or to reduce him to slavery if free. In Virginia an emancipated slave who had not left the state in the twelve months after being manumitted could be sold by the overseer of the poor "for the benefit of the Literary Fund"; similarly in North Carolina. In Florida a free mulatto or Negro could be made a slave for the smallest debt executed against him. In Mississippi any Negro or mulatto not being able to show himself a free man could be sold by the court as a slave. In Maryland (1717) any free Negro or mulatto, man or woman, intermarrying with a white person became a slave for life. Because the Negroes were brought in as slaves, the black color raised the presumption of slavery, which was generally extended to mulattoes, and in many states this presumption was enunciated by statute, putting on them the onus of proving that they were free. In Virginia and Kentucky one-fourth Negro blood constituted a presumption of slavery, and all children born of slave mothers were slaves.

Under the British West Indian and United States laws the Negro slave could not hope for self-redemption by purchase, and as slavery was assumed to be perpetual, there was only one route to freedom—manumission. But this route, if not entirely blocked, was made difficult by numerous impediments. The bias in favor of keeping the Negro in servitude contrasts with the other slave systems here under consideration, describes the explicit and the implicit test of the two systems, and foreshadows their ultimate outcome. For the attitude toward manumission is the crucial element in slavery; it implies the judgment of the moral status of the slave, and foreshadows his role in case of freedom.

Just as the favoring of manumission is perhaps the most characteristic and significant feature of the Latin-American slave system, so opposition to manumission and denial of opportunities for it are the primary aspect of slavery in the British West Indies and in the United States. The frequency and ease of manumission, more than any other factor, influence the character and ultimate outcome of the two slave systems in this hemisphere. For the ease of manumission bespeaks, even if only implicitly, a friendly attitude toward the person whose freedom is thus made possible and encouraged, just as the systematic obstruction of manumission implies a complete, if unconscious, attitude of hostility to those whose freedom is opposed or denied. And these contrasting attitudes toward manumission work themselves out in a hundred small, perhaps unnoticed, but significant details in the treatment of the Negro, both as a slave and when freed. Either policy reveals the bent of the system, and casts ahead of itself the long-run consequence of immediate practice and attitude.

2

# PREJUDICE AND SLAVERY

The Handlins had concluded, put crudely and without the many qualifications they demonstrated in their essay, that slavery preceded racial prejudice. A scholar whose chief interest lay in plumbing the nature of the American character, Carl N. Degler (1921- )—Coe Professor of American History at Stanford University—reversed the sequence in his analysis. Author of the influential general examination of American development, *Out of Our Past*, Degler has been particularly concerned to show the linkage between past and present. Most recently he has published a highly important examination of Brazilian and American slavery in a comparative perspective, *Neither Black nor White* (New York, 1971). In the following selection, Professor Degler takes direct issue with the Handlins.

It is indeed true as the Handlins in their article have emphasized that before the seventeenth century the Negro was rarely called a slave. But this fact should not overshadow the historical evidence which points to the institution without employing the name. Because no discriminatory title is placed upon the Negro we must not think that he was being treated like a white servant; for there is too much evidence to the contrary. Although the growth of a fully developed slave law was slow, unsteady and often unarticulated in surviving records, this is what one would expect when an institution is first being worked out. It is not the same, however, as saying that no slavery or discrimination against the Negro existed in the first decades of the Negro's history in America.

As will appear from the evidence which follows, the kinds of discrimination visited upon Negroes varied immensely. In the early 1640's it sometimes stopped short of lifetime servitude or inheritable status—the two attributes of true slavery—in other instances it included both. But regardless of the form of discrimination, the important point is that from the 1630's up until slavery clearly appeared in the statutes in the 1660's, the Negroes were being set apart and discriminated against as compared with the treatment accorded Englishmen, whether servants or free.

The colonists of the early seventeenth century were well aware of a distinction between indentured servitude and slavery. This is quite clear from the evidence in the very early years of the century. The most obvious means the English colonists had for learning of a different treatment for Negroes from that for white servants was the slave trade [1] and the slave systems of the Spanish and Portuguese colonies. As early as 1623, a voyager's book published in London indicated that Englishmen knew of the Negro as a slave in the South American colonies of Spain. The book told of the trade in "blacke people" who were "sold unto the Spaniard for him to carry into the West Indies, to remaine as slaves, either in their Mines or in any other servile uses, they in those countries put them to." In the phrase "remaine as slaves" is the element of unlimited service.

The Englishmen's treatment of another dark-skinned, non-Christian people—the Indians—further supports the argument that a special and inferior status was accorded the Negro virtually from the first arrival. Indian slavery was practised in all of the English settlements almost from the beginning and, though it received its impetus from the perennial wars between the races, the fact that an inferior and onerous service was established for the Indian makes it plausible to suppose that a similar status would be reserved for the equally different and pagan Negro.

The continental English could also draw upon other models of a differentiated status for Negroes. The earliest English colony to experiment with large numbers of Negroes in its midst was the shortlived settlement of Providence island, situated in the western Caribbean, just off the Mosquito Coast. By 1637, long before Barbados and the other British sugar islands utilized great numbers of Negroes, almost half of the population of this Puritan venture was black. Such a disproportion of races caused great alarm among the directors of the Company in London and repeated efforts were made to restrict the influx of blacks. Partly because of its large numbers of Negroes, Old Providence became well known to the mainland colonies of Virginia and New England. . . . Under such circumstances, it was to be expected that knowledge of the status accorded Negroes by these Englishmen would be transmitted to those on the mainland with whom they had such close and frequent contact.

Though the word "slave" is never applied to the Negroes on Providence, and only rarely the word "Servant," "Negroes," which was the term used, were obviously *sui generis;* they were people apart from the English. The Company, for example, distrusted them. "Association [Tortuga island] was deserted thro' their mutinous conduct," the Company told the Governor of Old Providence in 1637. "Further trade for them prohibited, with exceptions, until Providence be furnished with English." In another communication the Company again alluded to the dangers of "too great a number" of Negroes on the island and promised to send 200 English servants over to be exchanged for as many Negroes. A clearer suggestion of the difference in status between an English servant and a Negro is contained in the Company's letter announcing the forwarding of the 200 servants. As a further precaution against being overwhelmed by Negroes, it was ordered that a "family of fourteen"—which would include servants—was not to have more than six Negroes. "The surplusage may be sold to the poor men who have served their apprenticeship." But the Negroes, apparently, were serving for life.

Other British island colonies in the seventeenth century also provide evidence which is suggestive of this same development of a differing status for Negroes, even though the word "slave" was not always employed. Though apparently the first Negroes were only brought to Bermuda in 1617, as early as 1623 the Assembly passed an "Act to restrayne the insolencies of Negroes." The blacks were accused of stealing and of carrying "secretly cudgels, and other weapons and working tools." Such weapons, it was said, were "very dangerous and not meete to be suffered to be carried by such Vassals . . .". Already, in other words, Negroes were treated as a class apart. To reinforce this, Negroes were forbidden to "weare any weapon in the daytyme" and they were not to be outside or off their master's land during "any undue hours in the night tyme. . . ."

During the 1630's there were other indications that Negroes were treated as inferiors. As early as 1630 some Negroes' servitude was already slavery in that it was for life and inheritable. One Lew Forde possessed a Negro man, while the Company owned his wife; the couple had two children. Forde desired "to know which of the said children properly belong to himself and which to the Company." The Council gave him the older child and the Company received the other. A letter of Roger Wood in 1634 suggests that Negroes were already serving for life, for he asked to have a Negro, named Sambo, given to him, so that through the Negro "I or myne may *ever* be able" to carry on an old feud with an enemy who owned Sambo's wife.[2]

There is further evidence of discrimination against Negroes in later years. A grand jury in 1652 cited one Henry Gaunt as being "suspected of being unnecessarily conversant with negro women"—he had been giving them presents. The presentment added that "if he hath not left his familiarity with such creatures, it is desired that such abominations be inquired into, least the land mourne for them." The discrimination reached a high point in 1656 when the Governor proclaimed that "any Englishman" who discovered a Negro walking about at night without a pass, was empowered to "kill him then and theire without mercye." The proclamation further ordered that all free Negroes "shall be banished from these Islands, never to return eyther by purchase of any man, or otherwise. . . ." When some Negroes asked the Governor for their freedom in 1669, he denied they had any such claim, saying that they had been "purchased by" their masters "without condition or limitation. It being likewise soe practised in these American plantations and other parts of the world. . . ."

It is apparent, then, that the colonists on the mainland had ample opportunity before 1660 to learn of a different status for black men from that for Englishmen, whether servants or free.

From the evidence it would seem that the Englishmen in Virginia and Maryland learned their lesson well. This is true even though the sources available on the Negro's position in these colonies in the early years are not as abundant as I would like. It seems quite evident that the black man was set apart from the white on the continent just as he was being set apart in the island colonies. For example, in Virginia in 1630, one Hugh Davis was "soundly whipped before an Assembly of Negroes and others for abusing himself to the dishonor of God and the shame of Christians by defiling his body in lying with a negro." The unChristian-like character of such behavior was emphasized ten years later when Robert Sweet was ordered to do penance in Church for "getting a negro woman with child." An act passed in the Maryland legislature in 1639 indicated that at that early date the word "slave" was being applied to non-Englishmen. The act was an enumeration of the rights of "all Christian inhabitants (slaves excepted)." The slaves referred to could have been only Indians or Negroes, since all white servants were Christians. It is also significant of the differing treatment of the two races that though Maryland and Virginia very early in their history enacted laws fixing limits to the terms for servants who entered without written contracts, Negroes were never included in such protective provisions. The first of such laws was placed upon the books in 1639 in Maryland and 1643 in Virginia; in the Maryland statute, it was explicitly stated: "Slaves excepted."

In yet another way, Negroes and slaves were singled out for special status in the years before 1650. A Virginia law of 1640 provided that "all masters" should try to furnish arms to themselves and "all those of their families which shall be capable of arms"—which would include servants—"(excepting negros)." Not until 1648 did Maryland get around to such a prohibition, when it was provided that no guns should be given to "any Pagan for killing meate or to any other use," upon pain of a heavy fine.

At no time were white servants denied the right to bear arms; indeed, as these statutes inform us, they were enjoined to possess weapons.[3]

One other class of discriminatory acts against Negroes in Virginia and Maryland before 1660 also deserves to be noticed. Three different times before 1660—in 1643, 1644 and 1658—the Virginia assembly (and in 1654, the Maryilnd legislature) included Negro and Indian women among the "tithables." But white servant women were never placed in such a category, inasmuch as they were not expected to work in the fields. From the beginning, it would seem, Negro women, whether free or bond, were treated by the law differently from white women servants.

It is not until the 1640's that evidence of a status for Negroes akin to slavery, and, therefore, something more than mere discrimination begins to appear in the sources. Two cases of punishment for runaway servants in 1640 throw some light on the working out of a differentiated status for Negroes. The first case concerned three runaways, of whom two were white men and the third a Negro. All three were given thirty lashes, with the white men having the terms owed their masters extended a year, at the completion of which they were to work for the colony for three more years. The other, "being a Negro named John Punch shall serve his said master or his assigns for the time of his natural Life here or elsewhere." Not only was the Negro's punishment the most severe, and for no apparent reason, but he was, in effect, reduced to slavery. It is also clear, however, that up until the issuing of the sentence he must have had the status of a servant.

The second case, also of 1640, suggests that by that date some Negroes were already slaves. Six white men and a Negro were implicated in a plot to run away. The punishments meted out varied, but Christopher Miller "a dutchman" (a prime agent in the business) "was given the harshest treatment of all: thirty stripes, burning with an "R" on the cheek, a shackle placed on his leg for a year "and longer if said master shall see cause" and seven years of service for the colony upon completion of his time due his master. The only other one of the seven plotters to receive the stripes, the shackle and the "R" was the Negro Emanuel, but, significantly, he did not receive any sentence of work for the colony.

Presumably he was already serving his master for a life-time—*i.e.*, he was a slave. About this time in Maryland it does not seem to have been unusual to speak of Negroes as slaves, for in 1642 one "John Skinner mariner" agreed "to deliver unto . . . Leonard Calvert, fourteen negro-men-slaves and three women-slaves."

From a proceeding before the House of Burgesses in 1666 it appears that as early as 1644 that body was being called upon to determine who was a slave. The Journal of the House for 1666 reports that in 1644 a certain "mulata" bought "as a slave for Ever" was adjudged by the Assembly "no slave and but to serve as other Christian servants do and was freed in September 1665." Though no reason was given for the verdict, from the words "other Christian servants" it is possible that he was a Christian, for it was believed in the early years of the English colonies that baptism rendered a slave free. In any case, the Assembly uttered no prohibition of slavery as such and the owner was sufficiently surprised and aggrieved by the decision to appeal for recompense from the Assembly, even though the Negro's service was twenty-one years, an unheard of term for a "Christian servant."

In early seventeenth century inventories of estates, there are two distinctions which appear in the reckoning of the value of servants and Negroes. Uniformly, the Negroes were more valuable, even as children, than any white servant. Secondly, the naming of a servant is usually followed by the number of years yet remaining to his service; for the Negroes no such notation appears. Thus in an inventory in Virginia in 1643, a 22-year old white servant, with eight years still to serve, was valued at 1,000 pounds of tobacco, while a "negro boy" was rated at 3,000 pounds and a white boy with seven years to serve was listed as worth 700 pounds. An eight-year old Negro girl was calculated to be worth 2,000 pounds. On another inventory in 1655, two good men servants with four years to serve were rated at 1,300 pounds of tobacco, and a woman servant with only two years to go was valued at 800 pounds. Two Negro boys, however, who had no limit set to their terms, were evaluated at 4,100 pounds apiece, and a Negro girl was said to be worth 5,500 pounds.

These great differences in valuation of Negro and white "servants" strongly suggest, as does the failure to indicate term of service for the Negroes, that the latter were slaves at least in regard to life-time service. Beyond a question, there was some service which these blacks were rendering which enhanced their value—a service, moreover, which was not or could not be exacted from the whites. Furthermore, a Maryland deed of 1649 adumbrated slave status not only of life-time term, but of inheritance of status. Three Negroes "and all their issue both male and female" were deeded. . . .

Concurrently with these examples of onerous service or actual slavery of Negroes, there were of course other members of the race who did gain their freedom. But the presence of Negroes rising out of servitude to freedom does not destroy the evidence that others were sinking into slavery; it merely underscores the unsteady evolution of a slave status. The supposition that the practice of slavery long antedated the law is strengthed by the tangential manner in which recognition of Negro slavery first appeared in the Virginia statutes. It occurred in 1660 in a law dealing with punishments for runaway servants, where casual reference was made to those "negroes who are incapable of making satisfaction by addition of time," since they were already serving for life. . . .

As early as 1669 the Virginia law virtually washed its hands of protecting the Negro held as a slave. It allowed punishment of refractory slaves up to and including accidental death, relieving the master, explicitly, of any fear of prosecution, on the assumption that no man would "destroy his owne estate."

In fact by 1680 the law of Virginia had erected a high wall around the Negro. One discerns in the phrase "any negro or other slave" how the word "negro" had taken on the meaning of slave. Moreover, in the act of 1680 one begins to see the lineaments of the later slave codes. No Negro may carry any weapon of any kind, nor leave his master's ground without a pass, nor shall "any negroe or other slave . . . presume to lift his hand in opposition against any christian," and if a Negro runs away and reists recapture it "shalbe lawful for such person or persons to kill said negroe or slave. . . ."

Yet it would be a quarter of a century before Negroes would comprise even a fifth of the population of Virginia. Thus long before slavery or black labor became an important part of the Southern economy, a special and inferior status had been worked out for the Negroes who came to the English colonies. Unquestionably it was a demand for labor which dragged the Negro to American shores, but the status which he acquired here cannot be explained by reference to that economic motive. Long before black labor was as economically important as unfree white labor, the Negro had been consigned to a special discriminatory status which mirrored the social discrimination Englishmen practised against him. . . .

It would seem, then, that instead of slavery being the root of the discrimination visited upon the Negro in America, slavery was itself molded by the early colonists' discrimination against the outlander. In the absence of any law of slavery or commandments of the Church to the contrary—as was true of Brazil and Spanish-America—the institution of slavery into which the African was placed in the English colonies inevitably mirrored that discrimination and, in so doing, perpetuated it.

Once the English embodied their discrimination against the Negro in slave law, the logic of the law took over. Through the early eighteenth century, judges and legislatures in all the colonies elaborated the law among the discriminatory lines laid down in the amorphous beginnings. In doing so, of course, especially in the South, they had the added incentive of perpetuating and securing a labor system which by then had become indispensable to the economy. The cleavage between the races was in that manner deepened and hardened into the shape which became quite familiar by the nineteenth century. In due time, particularly in the South, the correspondence between the black man and slavery would appear so perfect that it would be difficult to believe that the Negro wa fitted for anything other than the degraded status in which he was almost always found. It would also be forgotten that the discrimination had begun long before slavery had come upon the scene.

## NOTES

1. The Handlins, "Origins of Southern Labor," . . . argue that the continental colonies could not have learned about a different status for Negroes from that of white servants from the slave trade because, they say, "the company of Royal Adventurers referred to their cargo as 'Negers,' 'Negro-servants,' 'Servants . . . from Africa,' or 'Negro Persons' but rarely as slaves." They overlook, however, abundant references to Negro slaves in the correspondence of the contemporary Royal African Company. Thus in 1663 a warrant for that company refers to "negro slaves" as a part of its monopoly. . . . In that same year the Privy Council wrote that the Spanish were "seeking to trade with our island of Barbada for a supply of Negro Slaves. . . ." And then the letter referred to a "supply of Negro Servants," and later still "for every Negro Person a Slave" and then "all such Negro Slaves" . . .
2. Emphasis added.
3. Handlin, "Origins of Southern Labor," . . . implies that these early restrictions were later repealed. "Until the 1660's," the Handlins write, "the statutes on the Negroes were not at all unique. Nor did they add up to a decided trend." In substantiation of this point they instance the "fluctuations" in the Negro's right to bear arms. Their cited evidence, however, does not sustain this generalization. Four references to the statutes of Virginia are made; of these four, only two deal with arms bearing. The first one, that referred to in the text above, indicates that Negroes were not to be armed. The other reference is at best an ambiguous statement about who is taxable and which of the taxables are to serve in the militia. It in no wise constitutes either a repeal or even a contradiction of the earlier statute, which, therefore, must be presumed to be

controlling. Their evidence for "fluctuations" in the right of Indians to bear arms suffers from the same weakness of sources. The two statutes they cite merely confirm the right of certain Indians to possess guns and deny them to other Indians. No "fluctuation" in rights is involved.

3

# CUBA AND VIRGINIA COMPARED

Tannenbaum had provided a basic outline of a theory but did not go on to examine in detail the ways in which slavery differed at the colonial or local level. Until many such studies of the actual functional, organic nature of slavery have been made, we will not understand the dynamics of the systems. One such study, comparing Cuba and Virginia, was the work of a Latin Americanist teaching at the University of Chicago, Herbert S. Klein (1936- ).

Virginia . . . developed a complete caste system, which essentially reinforced the slave system at all levels. Because of this seeming interdependence, the Virginia whites fought all attempts to destroy slavery, even when it was shown to be uneconomic, on the grounds that the system of slavery supported the now highly crucial pattern of race dominance. It was thus necessary for civil war and outside intervention to destroy slavery in the South. To the initial surprise of the southern whites themselves, however, the caste system had been so thoroughly implanted that it survived the destruction of slavery. Rapidly accommodating themselves to the new system of free labor, the Virginia whites were able to rework the labor base without seriously changing the position of the lower caste. For the augmented urban free-colored element, always a divisive factor in the caste arrangements even under slavery, the whites further developed their system of physical and economic segregation that had been initiated for the freedmen. This rapidly elaborated segregation system, which was highly developed even before the end of slavery, successfully obviated the potential threat of the urban free colored to stable race relations.[1]

It would, in fact, require the mass migration of the colored out of the South in the twentieth century to begin to modify this caste system. But even with this mass migration and the corresponding impact of urbanization, along with the integration of the Negro into the modern industrial labor force, the caste system has shown a surprising resiliency. Class differentiation finally began to appear on an important scale after 1900, but the "black bourgeoisie" has been prevented, until recently, from integrating into the system of social stratification that exists among the whites. Nor has a middle ground of mulatto assimilation been allowed to develop by which integration could be effected through miscegenation. The rules of color elaborated under slavery still operate today, defining a mulatto as a Negro and refusing to accept his as any meaningful alternative position.[2]

The Cuban slave system, on the other hand, did not support a caste arrangement, but in fact had been functioning in the last decades alongside a developing class system in which the free colored were actively participating. Cuba was progressively able to eliminate slavery when it was shown to Cuban planters that slave labor was no longer profitable. Already in the late 1830's planters had begun systematically to introduce both European and Yucatecan Indian contract laborers. And beginning in 1847 came the . . . importation of Chinese coolies, of whom over 124,000 would be introduced into the island by 1874, a figure far in excess of the most extreme estimates for illegal slave importations in this same period. Cuban planters were thus already heavily engaged in purchasing new forms of labor well before emancipation was formally adopted.

This whole voluntary reworking of the plantation labor force coincided with a major technical and structural reorganization of the sugar industry itself, which by the 1860's was the last major employer of slave labor.[3] Divesting themselves of expensive and now doubtfully remunerative slaves, progressive planters were freeing their capital by purchasing cheaper contract coolies or Yucatecans, or simply renting their slaves from others, and were heavily investing in a vast assortment of new machines, from steam engines to new boilers, which were being introduced on a large scale by the middle decades of the nineteenth century. The large planters were also cutting down their actual plantings and concentrating on the construction of major refineries, or *centrales*, which in turn needed far more cane than a single planter could economically produce on his own. By 1880, this whole restructuring process was leading both to the constant consolidation of sugar mills into giant full-time centrales and to the introduction on a large scale of smaller, independent, nonrefining growers on surrounding estates and even of sharecroppers on the larger plantations themselves.

Thus slavery was a dying institution even before the Ten Years' War (1868-78) erupted on the island and destroyed the very basis of the system. Primarily affecting the more traditional central and eastern portions of the island where slave labor was more entrenched, this first war for independence freed large numbers of slaves, who fought on both sides, and destroyed hundreds of sugar estates. At this same time, the progressive western section was going through . . . tremendous changes in structure and in labor . . . so that by the end of the war Cuba's sugar fields were being worked by a complex assortment of labor—from owned and rented slaves to coolie and Yucatecan contract laborers to white European and free-colored day workers and independent sharecroppers. The law of 1870 that began emancipation by retroactively freeing all slaves born after September, 1868, all persons who were over 60 or who would reach that age, and all slaves who had supported the royalist forces in the war was greeted with little opposition. It merely accelerated already established trends, and the slave population continued its rapid decline, dropping to 200,000 in 1877 and to but 150,000 by 1880. By this latter date the Spanish government finally decreed total abolition for the remaining adults with a tutelage system arranged to replace slavery, which in its turn was abolished in 1886.

When abolition finally came to Cuba, it thus affected an institution that had long ceased to play a vital part in any aspect of the economy. The sugar industry, its last significant stronghold, experienced little disruption with abolition, but continued its phenomenal expansion and modernization. Neither was there any major shortage of labor nor mass exodus to the cities, since a wage system was fully functioning on almost all the estates well before the end of slavery, and the new freedmen were easily absorbed into the vast pool of whites, older freedmen, and Chinese wage laborers, or into the independent sharecropper system.

All this clearly indicates that slavery for the Cuban whites was primarily a labor system that, when shown to be uneconomic, could be successfully abandoned by the planters. In Cuba there was no fear of emancipation changing racial relations, for the Cubans had long since accepted both racial miscegenation and an open-class system of social stratification. Even before slavery ended, economic and cultural attainments were becoming important elements in defining an individual's position in society, with color becoming more and more a secondary ranking tool.

Although after emancipation most full Negroes were initially found in the lower classes and the identification of color and class seemed quite strong, this was only a superficial relationship. Position in the class system of Cuba was never permanent, and social mobility was possible for even the darkest-skinned colored person. Within a few generations of emancipation increasing numbers of full colored were to be found in the middle classes, and as even before abolition, mulattoes were located at every level of society.

Equally important, Cuban society organized itself around a tripartite color system that permitted mulattoes to think of themselves and be accepted by both whites and Negroes as a distinct group, not participating in many of the "traits" and disabilities of the latter group. To be a mulatto usually meant more economic and social mobility. Also, given money and education, the mulatto even if *obscuro*, or very dark, would be ranked in the white category, and the corresponding Negro would be classified as mulatto, for in Cuba as in the rest of Latin America, "money whitened." This categorizing of the mulattoes as a distinct group also meant that for the Negro, interracial marriage could mean simply marrying up into the mulatto class, with the resulting lightening of his children being a major social and sometimes even economic asset in prerevolutionary Cuban society. With a multitude of subcategories being recognized within each of the three major areas, and with heavy miscegenation blurring color and features at either end of the mulatto scale, there was no crisis caused by "passing." Most often a person's "color" was more easily determined by his education and income than by any physical features he possessed.

This open quality of color definition has led to heavy miscegenation and to a massive movement between color categories on the part of the Cuban population. Each generation has seen the progressive decline of Negroes, despite a constant Negro immigration from Haiti and other Caribbean islands, and the progressive increase of mulattoes to the point that the majority of the Cuban colored now classify themselves by this term. While Negroes were passing into the mulatto category, mulattoes were continuously passing into the white group. Thus the percentage of total colored population has been steadily decreasing since the last decades of slavery, falling from 45.0% in 1861, to 26.8% in the census of 1953. This decline can only be explained in terms of a constant passing, since the growth rate of the colored population was internally as great as the white population and its own additions from immigration counterbalanced white immigration. As early as 1899, the Cuban colored had a slightly higher birth rate than Cuban whites and were far more urbanized, thus enjoying the same, if not better, health standards. Nor did any major immigration of whites occur, except from 1919 to 1931, and this was even offset by a heavy colored migration into the island accounting for one-quarter of the total immigrants. In fact, in 1943, foreigners made up 4% of both the white and the colored populations.

Thus the Cuban Negroes have been steadily moving into the majority mulatto grouping, and the mulattoes, in turn, have been defining themselves in ever larger numbers as whites. This process seems to be aiming toward a multicolored "white" population for the island, and in fact such an amalgamation process has already occurred with far smaller nuclei of colored populations in the La

Plata and Andean regions, where known colored populations of the colonial period have simply disappeared into a homogeneous and multishaded white population. . . .

. . . On the other hand, the heritage of North American slavery established patterns that were opposed to such a process of integration, and although these patterns have been seriously modified they continue to have an important impact on contemporary race relations.

## NOTES

1. The origin of segregation under slavery has been clearly demonstrated by Richard C. Wade, *Slavery in the Cities. The South* 1820-1860 (New York, 1964).
2. By this time the coffee industry was in total collapse, leaving the sugar industry as the only major plantation system functioning in Cuba. At the same time, with new slave imports ended, the process of coartación was causing a decline in urban slavery. Thus, between the censuses of 1841 and 1861 the number of slaves fell not only in absolute terms, but its percentage decline was even greater, going from 43% of the total population in the peak year of 1841 to but 29% of the population in 1861.

# 4

# THE PLANTATION AS A CONCENTRATION CAMP

Only one other work has been so influential on slave studies as that of Tannenbaum: Stanley M. Elkins' (1925- ) imaginative attempt to find some equations between the psychology induced in inmates of German prison and concentration camps during World War II and the psychological pressures upon Africans within the context of a New World plantation economy. Elkins' work was significant in several ways: he offered an explanation for why some Negro slaves may have chosen to play, quite consciously, the Sambo rôle that the traditional white Southerners thrust upon him; he thus provided an important addition to the body of literature that argues, convincingly, that environment rather than heredity plays the greater rôle in determining character. By drawing upon the work of sociologists and psychologists, he led other historians to see that they, too, might apply the insights and, on occasion, the methods of other disciplines to explain behavioral phenomena previously closed to historical inquiry. He also posed a test to the historical method itself, for his argument is by analogy, even an elaborate metaphor. To compare two institutions separated in time and place and by an enormous technological change is difficult enough, and the leap of faith necessary between data and conclusions was already great. Now an even greater, if more disciplined, leap would be required, for one needed not only to accept the data and conclusions of another body of scholars but also move, like Eliza upon the ice floes, from that body of scholarship to history without loss of credibility. There would be those who would argue, as we will see, that Elkins had not made the leap, but many would continue to find his contribution stimulating and important. His argument is a complex one but it will repay the close attention it demands.

. . . It will be assumed that there were elements in the very structure of the plantation system—its "closed" character—that could sustain infantilism as a normal feature of behavior. These elements, having less to do with "cruelty" per se than simply with the sanctions of authority, were effective and pervasive enough to require that such infantilism be characterized as something much more basic than mere "accommodations." It will be assumed that the sanctions of the system were in themselves sufficient to produce a recognizable personality type.

It should be understood that to identify a social type in this sense is still to generalize on a fairly crude level—and to insist for a limited purpose on the legitimacy of such generalizing is by no means to deny that, on more refined levels, a great profusion of individual types might have been observed in slave society. Nor need it be claimed that the "Sambo" type, even in the relatively crude sense employed here, was a universal type. It was, however, a plantation type, and a plantation existence embraced well over half the slave population. Two kinds of material will be used in the effort to picture the mechanisms whereby this adjustment to absolute power—an adjustment whose end product included infantile features of behavior—may have been effected. One is drawn from the theoretical knowledge presently available in social psychology, and the other, in the form of an analogy, is derived from some of the data that have come out of the German concentration camps. It is recognized in most theory that social behavior is regulated in some general ways by adjustment to symbols of authority—however diversely "authority" may be defined either in theory or in culture itself—and that such adjustment is closely related to the very formation of personality. A corollary would be, of course, that the more diverse these symbols of authority may be, the greater is the permissible variety of adjustment to them—and the wider the margin of individuality, consequently, in the development of the self. The question here has to do with the wideness or narrowness of that margin on the antebellum plantation.

The other body of material, involving an experience undergone by several million men and women in the concentration camps of our own time, contains certain items of relevance to the problem here being considered. The experience was analogous to that of slavery and was one in which wide-scale instances of infantilization were observed. The material is sufficiently detailed, and sufficiently documented by men who not only took part in the experience itself but who were versed in the use of psychological theory for analyzing it, that the advantages of drawing upon such data for purposes of analogy seem to outweigh the possible risks.

The introduction of this second body of material must to a certain extent govern the theoretical strategy itself. It has been recognized both implicitly and explicitly that the psychic impact and effects of the concentration-camp experience were not anticipated in existing theory and that consequently such theory would require some major supplementation. . . . The experience showed, in any event, that infantile personality features could be induced in a relatively short time among large numbers of adult human beings coming from very diverse backgrounds. The particular strain which was thus placed upon prior theory consisted in the need to make room not only for the cultural and environmental sanctions that sustain personality (which in a sense Freudian theory already had) but also for a virtually unanticipated problem: actual change in the personality of masses of adults. It forced a reappraisal and new appreciation of how completely and effectively prior cultural sanctions for behavior and personality could be detached to make way for new and different sanctions, and of how adjustments could be made by individuals to a species of authority vastly different from any previously known. The revelation for theory was the process of detachment.

These cues, accordingly, will guide the argument on Negro slavery. Several million people were detached with a peculiar effectiveness from a great variety of cultural backgrounds in Africa —a detachment operating with infinitely more effectiveness upon those brought to North America than upon those who came to Latin America. It was achieved partly by the shock experience inherent in the very mode of procurement but more specifically by the type of authority-system to which they were introduced and to which they had to adjust for physical and psychic survival. The new adjustment, to absolute power in a closed system, involved infantilization, and the detachment was so complete that little trace of prior (and thus alternative) cultural sanctions for behavior and personality remained for the descendants of the first generation. For them, adjustment to clear and omnipresent authority could be more or less automatic—as much so, or as little, as it is for anyone whose adjustment to a social system begins at birth and to whom that system represents normality. We do not know how generally a full adjustment was made by the first generation of fresh slaves from Africa. But we do know—from a modern experience—that such an adjustment is possible, not only within the same generation but within two or three years. This proved possible for people in a full state of complex civilization, for men and women who were not black and not savages. . . .

The immense relation [*sic* for revelation] for psychology in the concentration-camp literature has been the discovery of how elements of dramatic personality change could be brought about in masses of individuals. And yet it is not proper that the crude fact of "change" alone should dominate the conceptual image with which one emerges from this problem. "Change" per se, change that does not go beyond itself, is productive of nothing; it leaves only destruction, shock, and howling bedlam behind it unless some future basis of stability and order lies waiting to guarantee it and give it reality. So it is with the human psyche, which is apparently capable of making terms with a state other than liberty as we know it. The very dramatic features of the process just described may upset the nicety of this point. There is the related danger, moreover, of unduly stressing the individual psychology of the problem at the expense of its social psychology.

These hazards might be minimized by maintaining a conceptual distinction between two phases of the group experience. The process of detachment from prior standards of behavior and value is one of them, and is doubtless the more striking, but there must be another one. That such detachment can, by extension, involve the whole scope of an individual's culture is an implication for which the vocabulary of individual psychology was caught somewhat unawares. Fluctuations in the state of the individual psyche could formerly be dealt with, or so it seemed, while taking for granted the more or less static nature of social organization, and with a minimum of reference to its features. That such organization might itself become an important variable was therefore a possibility not highly developed in theory, focused as theory was upon individual case histories to the invariable minimization of social and cultural setting. The other phase of the experience should be considered as the "stability" side of the problem, that phase which stabilized what the "shock" phase only opened the way for. This was essentially a process of adjustment to a standard of social normality, though in this case a drastic *re*adjustment and compressed within a very short time—a process which under typical conditions of individual and group existence is supposed to begin at birth and last a lifetime and be transmitted in many and diffuse ways from generation to generation. The adjustment is assumed to be slow and organic, and it normally is. Its numerous aspects extend much beyond psychology; those aspects have in the past been treated at great leisure within the rich provinces not only of psychology but of history, sociology, and literature as well. What rearrangement and compression of these provinces may be needed to accommodate a mass experience that not only involved profound individual shock but also required rapid assimilation to a drastically different form of social organization, can hardly be known. But perhaps the most conservative beginning may be made with existing psychological theory.

The theoretical system whose terminology was orthodox for most of the Europeans who have written about the camps was that of Freud. It was necessary for them to do a certain amount of improvising, since the scheme's existing framework provided only the narrowest leeway for dealing with such radical concepts as out-and-out change in personality. This was due to two kinds of limitations which the Freudian vocabulary places upon the notion of the "self." One is that the superego—that part of the self involved in social relationships, social values, expectations of others, and so on—is conceived as only a small and highly refined part of the "total" self. The other is the assumption that the content and character of the superego is laid down in childhood and undergoes relatively little basic alteration thereafter. Yet a Freudian diagnosis of the concentration-camp inmate—whose social self, or superego, did appear to change and who seemed basically changed thereby—is, given these limitations, still possible. Elie Cohen, whose analysis is the most thorough of these, specifically states that "the superego acquired new values in a concentration camp." The old values, according to Dr. Cohen, were first silenced by the shocks which produced "acute depersonalization" (the subject-object split: "It is not the real 'me' who is undergoing this"), and by the powerful drives of hunger and survival. Old values, thus set aside, could be replaced by new ones. It was a process made possible by "infantile regression"—regression to a previous condition of childlike dependency in which parental prohibitions once more became all-powerful and in which parental judgments might once more be internalized. In this way a new "father-image," personified in the SS guard, came into being. That the prisoner's identification with the SS could be so positive is explained by still another mechanism: the principle of "identification with the aggressor." "A child," as Anna Freud writes, "interjects some characteristic of an anxiety-object and so assimilates an anxiety-experience which he has just undergone. . . . By impersonating the aggressor, assuming his attributes or imitating his aggression, the child transforms himself from the person threatened into the person who makes the threat." In short, the child's only "defense" in the presence of a cruel, all-powerful father is the psychic defense of identification.

Now one could, still retaining the Freudian language, represent all this in somewhat less cumbersome terms by a slight modification of the metaphor. It could simply be said that under great stress the superego, like a bucket, is violently emptied of content and acquires, in a radically changed setting, new content. It would thus not be necessary to postulate a literal "regression" to childhood in order for this to occur. . . .

A second theoretical scheme is better prepared for crisis and more closely geared to social environment than the Freudian adaptation indicated above, and it may consequently be more suitable for accommodating not only the concentration-camp experience but also the more general problem of plantation slave personality. This is the "interpersonal theory" developed by the late Harry Stack Sullivan. One may view this body of work as the response to a peculiarly American set of needs. The system of Freud, so aptly designed for a European society the stability of whose institutional and status relationships could always to a large extent be taken for granted, turns out to be less clearly adapted to the culture of the United States. The American psychiatrist has had to deal with individuals in a culture where the diffuse, shifting, and often uncertain quality of such relationships has always been more pronounced than in Europe. He has come to appreciate the extent to which these relationships actually support the individual's psychic balance—the full extent, that is, to which the self is "social" in its nature. Thus a psychology whose terms are flexible enough to permit altering social relationships to make actual differences in character structure would be a psychology especially promising for dealing with the present problem.

Sullivan's great contribution was to offer a concept whereby the really critical determinants of personality might be isolated for purposes of observation. Out of the hopelessly immense totality of "influences" which in one way or another go to make up the personality, or "self," Sullivan designated one—the estimations and expectations of others—as the one promising to unlock the most secrets. He then made a second elimination: the *majority* of "others" in one's existence may for theoretical purposes be neglected; what counts is who the *significant* others are. Here, "significant others" [1] may be understood very crudely to mean those individuals who hold, or seem to hold, the keys to security in one's own personal situation, whatever its nature. Now as to the psychic processes whereby these "significant others" become an actual part of the personality, it may be said that the very sense of "self" first emerges in connection with anxiety about the attitudes of the most important persons in one's life (initially, the mother, father, and their surrogates—persons of more or less absolute authority), and automatic attempts are set in motion to adjust to these attitudes. In this way their approval, their disapproval, their estimates and appraisals, and indeed a whole range of their expectations become as it were internalized, and are reflected in one's very character. Of course as one "grows up," one acquires more and more significant others whose attitudes are diffuse and may indeed compete, and thus "significance," in Sullivan's sense, becomes subtler and less easy to define. The personality exfoliates; it takes on traits of distinction and, as we say, "individuality." The impact of particular significant others is less dramatic than in early life. But the pattern is a continuing one; new significant others do still appear, and theoretically it is conceivable that even in mature life the personality might be visibly affected by the arrival of such a one—supposing that this new significant other were vested with sufficient authority and power. In any event there are possibilities for fluidity and actual change inherent in this concept which earlier schemes have lacked.

The purest form of the process is to be observed in the development of children, not so much because of their "immaturity" as such (though their plasticity is great and the imprint of early experience goes deep), but rather because for them there are fewer signficant others. For this reason—because the pattern is simpler and more easily controlled—much of Sullivan's attention was devoted to what happens in childhood. In any case let us say that unlike the adult, the child, being drastically limited in the selection of significant others, must operate in a "closed system."

Such are the elements which make for order and balance in the normal self: "significant others" plus "anxiety" in a special sense—conceived with not simply disruptive but also guiding, warning functions. The structure of "interpersonal" theory thus has considerable room in it for conceptions of guided change—

change for either beneficent or malevolent ends. One technique for managing such change would of course be the orthodox one of psychoanalysis; another, the actual changing of significant others. . . .

Consider the camp prisoner—not the one who fell by the wayside but the one who was eventually to survive; consider the ways in which he was forced to adjust to the one significant other which he now had—the SS guard, who held absolute dominion over every aspect of his life. The very shock of his introduction was perfectly designed to dramatize this fact; he was brutally maltreated ("as by a cruel father"); the shadow of resistance would bring instant death. Daily life in the camp, with its fear and tension, taught over and over the lesson of absolute power. It prepared the personality for a drastic shift in standards. It crushed whatever anxieties might have been drawn from prior standards; such standards had become meaningless. It focused the prisoner's attention constantly on the moods, attitudes, and standards of the only man who mattered. A truly childlike situation was thus created: utter and abject dependency on one, or on a rigidly limited few, significant others. All the conditions which in normal life would give the individual leeway—which allowed him to defend himself against a new and hostile significant other, no matter how powerful—were absent in the camp. No competition of significant others was possible; the prisoner's comrades for practical purposes were helpless to assist him.[2] He had no degree of independence, no lines to the outside, in any matter. Everything, every vital concern, focused on the SS: food, warmth, security, freedom from pain, all depended on the omnipotent significant other, all had to be worked out within the closed system. Nowhere was there a shred of privacy; everything one did was subject to SS supervision. The pressure was never absent. It is thus no wonder that the prisoners should become "as children." It is no wonder that their obedience became unquestioning, that they did not revolt, that they could not "hate" their masters. Their masters' attitudes had become *internalized* as a part of their very selves; those attitudes and standards now dominated all others that they had. They had, indeed, been "changed."

There still eixsts a third conceptual framework within which these phenomena may be considered. It is to be found in the growing field of "role psychology." This psychology is not at all incompatible with interpersonal theory; the two might easily be fitted into the same system. But it might be strategically desirable, for several reasons, to segregate them for purposes of discussion. One such reason is the extraordinary degree to which role psychology shifts the focus of attention upon the individual's cultural and institutional environment rather than upon his "self." At the same time it gives us a manageable concept—that of "role"—for mediating betwen the two. As a mechanism, the role enables us to isolate the unique contribution of culture and institutions toward maintaining the psychic balance of the individual. In it, we see formalized for the individual a range of choices in models of behavior and expression, each with its particular style, quality, and attributes. The relationship between the "role" and the "self," though not yet clear, is intimate; it is at least possible at certain levels of inquiry to look upon the individual as the variable and upon the roles extended him as the stable factor. We thus have a potentially durable link between individual psychology and the study of culture. . . .

Let us note certain of the leading terms.[3] A "social role" is definable in its simplest sense as the behavior expected of persons specifically located in specific social groups. A distinction is kept between "expectations" and "behavior"; the expectations of a role (embodied in the "script") theoretically exist in advance and are defined by the organization, the institution, or by society at large. Behavior (the "performance") refers to the manner in which the role is played. Another distinction involves roles which are "pervasive" and those which are "limited." A pervasive role is extensive in scope ("female cittizen") and not only influences but also sets bounds upon the other sorts of roles available to the individual ("mother," "nurse," but not "husband," "soldier"); a limited role ("purchaser," "patient") is transitory and intermittent. A further concept is that of "role clarity." Some roles are more specifically defined than others; their impact upon performance (and, indeed, upon the personality of the performer) depends on the clarity of their definition. Finally, it is asserted that those roles which carry with them the clearest and most automatic rewards and punishments are those which will be (as it were) most "artistically" played.

What sorts of things might this explain? It might illuminate the process whereby the child develops his personality in terms not only of the roles which his parents offer him but of those which he "picks up" elsewhere and tries on. It could show how society, in its coercive character, lays down patterns of behavior with which it expects the individual to comply. It suggests the way in which society, now turning its benevolent face to the individual, tenders him alternatives and defines for him the style appropriate to their fulfilment. It provides us with a further term for the definition of personality itself; there appears an extent to which we can say that personality is actually made up of the roles which the individual plays. And here, once more assuming "change" to be possible, we have in certain ways the least cumbersome terms for plotting its course.

The application of the model to the concentration camp should be simple and obvious. What was expected of the man entering the role of camp prisoner was laid down for him upon arrival:

> "Here you are not in a penitentiary or prison but in a place of instruction. Order and discipline are here the highest law. If you ever want to see freedom again, you must submit to a severe training. . . . But woe to those who do not obey our iron discipline. Our methods are thorough! Here there is no compromise and no mercy. The slightest resistance will be ruthlessly suppressed. Here we sweep with an iron broom!" [4]

Expectation and performance must coincide exactly; the lines were to be read literally; the missing of a single cue meant extinction. The role was pervasive; it vetoed any other role and smashed all prior ones. "Role clarity"—and clarity here was blinding; its definition was burned into the prisoner by every detail of his existence:

> In normal life the adult enjoys a certain measure of independence; within the limits set by society he has a considerable measure of liberty. Nobody orders him when and what to eat, where to take up his residence or what to wear, neither to take his rest on Sunday nor when to have his bath, nor when to go to bed. He is not beaten during his work, he need not ask permission to go to the W.C., he is not continually kept on the run, he does not feel that the work he is doing is silly or childish, he is not confined behind barbed wire, he is not counted twice a day or more, he is not left unprotected against the actions of his fellow citizens, he looks after his family and the education of his children.
>
> How altogether different was the life of the concentration-camp prisoner! What to do during each part of the day was arranged for him, and decisions were made about him from which there was no appeal. He was impotent and suffered from bedwetting, and because of his chronic diarrhea he soiled his underwear. . . . The dependence of the prisoner on the SS . . . may be compared to the dependence of children on their parents. . . .[5]

The impact of this role, coinciding as it does in a hundred ways with that of the child, has already been observed. Its rewards were brutally simple—life rather than death; its punishments were automatic. By the survivors it was—it had to be—a role *well played*.

Nor was it simple, upon liberation, to shed the role. Many of the inmates, to be sure, did have prior roles which they could resume, former significant others to whom they might reorient themselves, a repressed superego which might once more be resurrected. To this extent they were not "lost souls." But to the extent that their entire personalities, their total selves, had been involved in this experience, to the extent that old arrangements had been disrupted, that society itself had been overturned while they had been away, a "return" was fraught with innumerable obstacles.

It is hoped that the very hideousness of a special example of slavery has not disqualified it as a test for certain features of a far milder and more benevolent form of slavery. But it should still be possible to say, with regard to the individuals who lived as slaves within the respective systems, that just as on one level there is every difference between a wretched childhood and a carefree one, there are, for other purposes, limited features which the one may be said to have shared with the other.

Both were closed systems from which all standards based on prior connections had been effectively detached. A working adjustment to either system required a childlike conformity, a limited choice of "significant others." Cruelty per se cannot be considered the primary key to this; of far greater importance was the simple "closedness" of the system, in which all lines of authority descended from the master and in which alternative social bases that might have supported alternative standards were systematically suppressed.[6] The individual, consequently, for his very psychic security, had to picture his master in some way as the "good father," even when, as in the concentration camp, it made no sense at all. But why should it not have made sense for many a simple plantation Negro whose master did exhibit, in all the ways that could be expected, the features of the good father who was really "good"? If the concentration camp could produce in two or three years the results that it did, one wonders how much more pervasive must have been those attitudes, expectations, and values which had, certainly, their benevolent side and which were accepted and transmitted over generations.

For the Negro child, in particular, the plantation offered no really satisfactory father-image other than the master. The "real" father was virtually without authority over his child since discipline, parental responsibility, and control of rewards and punishments all rested in other hands; the slave father could not even protect the mother of his children except by appealing directly to the master. Indeed, the mother's own role loomed far larger for the slave child than did that of the father. She controlled those few activities—household care, preparation of food, and rearing of children—that were left to the slave family. For that matter, the very etiquette of plantation life removed even the honorific attributes of fatherhood from the Negro male, who was addressed as "boy"—until, when the vigorous years of his prime were past, he was allowed to assume the title of "uncle."

From the master's viewpoint, slaves had been defined in law as property, and the master's power over his property must be absolute. But then this property was still human property. These slaves mighet never be quite as human as *he* was, but still there were certain standards that could be laid down for their behavior: obedience, fidelity, humility, docility, cheerfulness, and so on. Industry and diligence would of course be demanded, but a final element in the master's situation would undoubtedly qualify that expectation. Absolute power for him meant absolute dependency for the slave—the dependency not of the developing child but of the perpetual child. For the master, the role most aptly fitting such a relationship would naturally be that of the father. As a father he could be either harsh or kind, as he chose, but as a *wise* father he would have, we may suspect, a sense of the limits of his situation. He must be ready to cope with *all* the qualities of the child, exasperating as well as ingratiating. He might conceivably have to expect in this child—besides his loyalty, docility, humility, cheerfulness, and (under supervision) his diligence—such additional qualities as irresponsibility, playfulness, silliness, laziness, and (quite possibly) tendencies to lying and stealing. Should the entire prediction prove accurate, the result would be something resembling "Sambo."

The social and psychological sanctions of role-playing may in the last analysis prove to be the most satisfactory of the several approaches to Sambo, for, without doubt, of all the roles in American life that of Sambo was by far the most pervasive. The outlines of the role might be sketched in by crude necessity, but what of the finer shades? The sanctions against overstepping it were bleak enough, but the rewards—the sweet applause, as it were, for performing it with sincerity and feeling—were something to be appreciated on quite another level. The law, untuned to the deeper harmonies, could command the player to be present for the occasion, and the whip might even warn against his missing the grosser cues, but could those things really insure the performance that melted all hearts? Yet there was many and many a performance, and the audiences (whose standards were high) appear to have been for the most part well pleased. They were actually viewing their own masterpiece. Much labor had been lavished upon this chef d'oeuvre, the most genial resources of Southern society had been available for the work; touch after touch had been applied throughout the years, and the result—embodied not in the unfeeling law but in the richest layers of Southern lore—had been the product of an exquisitely rounded collective creativity. And indeed, in a sense that somehow transcended the merely ironic, it was a labor of love. "I love the simple and unadulterated slave, with his geniality, his mirth, his swagger, and his nonsense," wrote Edward Pollard. "I love to look upon his countenance shining with content and grease; I love to study his affectionate heart; I love to mark that peculiarity in him, which beneath all his buffoonery exhibits him as a creature of the tenderest sensibilities, mingling his joys and his sorrows with those of his master's home.[7] Love, even on those terms, was surely no inconsequential reward.

But what were the terms? The Negro was to be a child forever. "The Negro . . . in his true nature, is always a boy, let him be ever so old. . . ." "He is . . . a dependent upon the white race; dependent for guidance and direction even to the procurement of his most indispensable necessaries. Apart from this protection he has the helplessness of a child—without foresight, without faculty of contrivance, without thrift of any kind." [8] Not only was he a child; he was a happy child. Few Southern writers failed to describe with obvious fondness the bubbling gaiety of a plantation holiday or the perpetual good humor that seemed to mark the Negro character, the good humor of an everlasting childhood.

The role, of course, must have been rather harder for the earliest generations of slaves to learn. . . .

Might the process, on the other hand, be reversed? It is hard to imagine its being reversed overnight. The same role might still be played in the years after slavery—we are told that it was [9]—

and yet it was played to more vulgar audiences with cruder standards, who paid much less for what they saw. The lines might be repeated more and more mechanically, with less and less conviction; the incentives to perfection could become hazy and blurred, and the excellent old piece could degenerate over time into low farce. There could come a point, conceivably, with the old zest gone, that it was no longer worth the candle. The day might come at last when it dawned on a man's full waking consciousness that he had really grown up, that he was, after all, only playing a part. . . .

Why should it be, turning . . . to Latin America, that there one finds no Sambo, no social tradition, that is, in which slaves were defined by virtually complete consensus as children incapable of being trusted with the full privileges of freedom and adulthood? There, the system surely had its brutalities. The slaves arriving there from Africa had also undergone the capture, the sale, the Middle Passage. They too had been uprooted from a prior culture, from a life very different from the one in which they now found themselves. There, however, the system was not closed.

Here again the concentration camp, paradoxically enough, can be instructive. There were in the camps a very small minority of the survivors who had undergone an experience different in crucial ways from that of the others, an experience which protected them from the full impact of the closed system. These people, mainly by virtue of wretched little jobs in the camp administration which offered them a minute measure of privilege, were able to carry on "underground" activities. In a practical sense the actual operations of such "undergrounds" as were possible may seem to us unheroic and limited: stealing blankets; "organizing" a few bandages, a little medicine, from the camp hospital; black market arrangements with a guard for a bit of extra food and protection for oneself and one's comrades; the circulation of news; and other such apparently trifling activities. But for the psychological balance of those involved, such activities were vital; they made possible a fundamentally different adjustment to the camp. To a prisoner so engaged, there were others who mattered, who gave real point to his existence—the SS was no longer the *only* one. Conversely, the role of the child was not the only one he played.

He could take initiative; he could give as well as receive protection; he did things which had meaning in adult terms. He had, in short, alternative roles; this was a fact which made such a prisoner's transition from his old life to that of the camp less agonizing and destructive; those very prisoners, moreover, appear to have been the ones who could, upon liberation, resume normal lives most easily. . . .

It was just such a difference—indeed, a much greater one—that separated the typical slave in Latin America from the typical slave in the United States. Though he too had experienced the Middle Passage, he was entering a society where alternatives were significantly more diverse than those awaiting his kinsman in North America. Concerned in some sense with his status were distinct and at certain points competing institutions. This involved multiple and often competing "significant others." His master was, of course, clearly the chief one—but not the only one. There could, in fact, be a considerable number: the friar who boarded his ship to examine his conscience, the confessor; the priest who made the rounds and who might report irregularities in treatment to the *procurador;* the zealous Jesuit quick to resent a master's intrusion upon such sacred matters as marriage and worship (a resentment of no small consequence to the master); the local magistrate, with his eye on the fling's official protector of slaves, who would find himself in trouble were the laws too widely evaded; the king's informer who received one-third of the fines. For the slave the result was a certain latitude; the lines did not all converge on one man; the slave's personality, accordingly, did not have to focus on a single role. He was, true enough, primarily a slave. Yet he might in fact perform multiple roles. He could be a husband and a father (for the American slave these roles had virtually no meaning); open to him also were such activities as artisan, peddler, petty merchant, truck gardener (the law reserved to him the necessary time and a share of the proceeds, but such arrangements were against the law for Sambo); he could be a communicant in the church, a member of a religious fraternity (roles guaranteed by the most powerful institution in Latin America—comparable privileges in the American South depended on a master's pleasure.) These roles were all legitimized and protected *outside* the plantation; they offered a diversity of channels for the development of personality. Not only did the individual have multiple roles open to him as a slave, but the very nature of these roles made possible a certain range of aspirations should he some day become free. He could have a fantasy-life not limited to catfish and watermelons; it was within his conception to become a priest, an independent farmer, a successful merchant, a military officer. The slave could actually—to an extent quite unthinkable in the United States—conceive of himself *as a rebel.* Bloody slave revolts, actual wars, took place in Latin America; nothing on this order occurred in the United States.[10] But even without a rebellion, society here had a network of customary arrangements, rooted in antiquity, which made possible at many points a smooth transition of status from slave to free and which provided much social space for the exfoliation of individual character.

To the typical slave on the ante-bellum plantation in the United States, society of course offered no such alternatives. But that is hardly to say that something of an "underground"—something rather more, indeed, than an underground—could not exist in Southern slave society. And there were those in it who hardly fitted the picture of "Sambo."

The American slave system, compared with that of Latin America, was closed and circumscribed, but, like all social systems, its arrangements were less perfect in practice than they appeared to be in theory. It was possible for significant numbers of slaves, in varying degrees, to escape the full impact of the system and its coercions upon personality. The house servant, the urban mechanic, the slave who arranged his own employment and paid his master a stipulated sum each week, were all figuratively members of the "underground." Even among those working on large plantations, the skilled craftsman or the responsible slave foreman had a measure of independence not shared by his simpler brethren. Even the single slave family owned by a small farmer had a status much closer to that of house servants than to that of a plantation labor gang. For all such people there was a margin of space denied to the majority; the system's authority-structure claimed their bodies but not quite their souls. . . .

It is of great interest to note that although the danger of slave revolts . . . was much overrated by touchy Southerners; the revolt that actually did occur were in no instance planned by plantation laborers but rather by Negroes whose qualities of leadership were developed well outside the full coercions of the plantation authority-system. Gabriel, who led the revolt of 1800, was a blacksmith who lived a few miles outside Richmond; Denmark Vesey, leading spirit of the 1822 plot at Charleston, was a freed Negro artisan who had been born in Africa and served several years aboard a slave-trading vessel; and Nat Turner, the Virginia slave who fomented the massacre of 1831, was a literate preacher of recognized intelligence. Of the plots that have been convincingly substantiated (whether they came to anything or not), the majority originated in urban centers. . . .

## NOTES

1. Sullivan refined this concept from the earlier notion of the "generalized other" formulated by George Herbert Mead. "The organized community or social group [Mead wrote] which gives to the individual his unity of self may be called 'the generalized other.' The attitude of the generalized other is the attitude of the whole community. Thus, for example, in the case of such a social group as a ball team, the team is the generalized other in so far as it enters—as an organized process or social activity—into the experience of any one of the individual members of it." George H. Mead, *Mind, Self and Society: From the Standpoint of a Social Behaviorist* (Chicago, 1934), p. 154.
2. It should be noted that there were certain important exceptions. . . .
3. In this paragraph I duplicate and paraphrase material from Eugene and Ruth Hartley, *Fundamentals of Social Psychology* (New York, 1952), chap. xvi. See also David C. McClelland, *Personality* (New York, 1951), pp. 289-332. Both these books

are, strictly speaking, "texts," but this point could be misleading, inasmuch as the whole subject is one not normally studied at an "elementary" level anywhere. . . .

4. Quoted in Leon Szalet, *Experiment "E"* (New York, 1945), p. 138.
5. Elie Cohen, *Human Behavior in the Concentration Camp*, (London, 1954), pp. 173-74.
6. The experience of American prisoners taken by the Chinese during the Korean War seems to indicate that profound changes in behavior and values, if not in basic personality itself, can be effected without the use of physical torture or extreme deprivation. The Chinese were able to get large numbers of Americans to act as informers and to co-operate in numerous ways in the effort to indoctrinate all the prisoners with Communist propaganda. The technique contained two key elements. One was that all formal and informal authority structures within the group were systematically destroyed; this was done by isolating officers, non-commissioned officers, and any enlisted men who gave indications of leadership capacities. The other element involved the continual emphasizing of the captors' power and influence by judicious manipulation of petty rewards and punishments and by subtle hints of the greater rewards and more severe punishments (repatriation or non-repatriation) that rested with the pleasure of those in authority. See Edgar H. Schein, "Some Observations on Chinese Methods of Handling Prisoners of War," *Public Opinion Quarterly*, XX (Spring, 1956), 321-27.
7. Edward A. Pollard, *Black Diamonds Gathered in the Darkey Homes of the South* (New York, 1859), p. 58.
8. [Mark Littleton] John Pendleton Kennedy, *Swallow Barn* (Philadelphia, 1832) [II, 469].
9. Even Negro officeholders during Reconstruction, according to Francis B. Simkins, "were known to observe carefully the etiquette of the Southern caste system." "New Viewpoints of Southern Reconstruction," *Journal of Southern History*, V (Feb., 1939), 52.
10. Compared with the countless uprisings of the Brazilian Negroes, the slave revolts in our own country appear rather

desperate and futile. Only three emerge as worthy of any note, and their seriousness—even when described by a sympathetic historian like Herbert Aptheker—depends largely on the supposed plans of the rebels rather than on the things they actually did. The best organized of such "revolts," those of [Denmark] Vesey and Gabriel, were easily suppressed, while the most dramatic of them—the Nat Turner Rebellion—was characterized by little more than aimless butchery. The Brazilian revolts, on the other hand, were marked by imagination and a sense of direction, and they often involved large-scale military operations. One is impressed both by their scope and their variety. They range from the legendary Palmares Republic of the seventeenth century (a Negro state organized by escaped slaves and successfully defended for over fifty years), to the bloody revolts of the Moslem Negroes of Bahia which, between 1807 and 1835, five times paralyzed a substantial portion of Brazil. Many such wars were launched from the *quilombos* . . . ; there were also the popular rebellions in which the Negroes of an entire area would take part. One is immediately struck by the heroic stature of the Negro leaders: no allowances of any sort need be made for them; they are impressive from any point of view. . . . Their brilliance, gallantry, and warlike accomplishments give to their histories an almost legendary quality. . . .

# 5

## SLAVERY AMONGST THE MUSLIMS OF AFRICA

African Studies have not developed extensively enough for the emergence of a full and clear picture of the nature of pre-European African slavery. Rather more evidence is available concerning the effects of European and New World slave trading upon the indigenous forms of African slavery which had preceded the wide-scale commercialization of the trade, but much research remains to be done in this area as well. A group of scholars, originally organized by Professor Roger Anstey of the University of Kent, in Canterbury, England, have begun a careful reassessment of the economics of the slave trade itself, just as Philip D. Curtin has recently published a close argument on the numbers of Africans actually transported to the New World during the pre-1807 trade: *The Atlantic Slave Trade: A Census* (Madison, Wisc., 1969). In Britain, Dr. J. R. Goody and others, of the African Studies Centre in the University of Cambridge and at the London School of Economics, currently are engaged in a broadly-based re-examination of comparative slave systems, with emphasis being placed upon a cross-cultural perspective for African slavery in particular. Until such work is completed, however, one must turn to somewhat more impressionistic accounts which, in themselves, are forced to rely upon the impressions of European travellers. One of the best statements of the great variety to be found in the domestic treatment of slaves in Muslim Africa, a statement which by implication throws light on the varying natures of slavery before as well as after the opening of Africa to Europeans, is by Allan G. B. (1895- ) and Humphrey J. Fisher, father and son, who wrote on *Slavery and Muslim Society in Africa*. Allan Fisher was with the International Monetary Fund until his retirement in 1960, while Humphrey Fisher is on the staff of the School of Oriental and African Studies of the University of London.

The fate of a slave who survived a raid upon his (or her) home, and the rigours of the journeys which then had to be made, naturally varied very widely. Some peoples accepted enslavement more easily than others: the eastern Arabs said that slaves from Ulungu quickly became unmanageable, dull and morose, and many committed suicide, a measure rarely adopted by other peoples in that area; again, slaves from Okrika in eastern Nigeria

> have always proved refractory and incorrigible, and have often died broken-hearted, offering little or no encourageemnt to buyers to recruit their ranks with substitutes from that place.

Some areas were more dispiriting than others: slaves isolated on the island of San Tome sometimes ate earth for suicide. . . .

"Everywhere," [Gustav] Nachtigal observed, "Islam brings with it a mild administration of the institution of slavery." Especially in Fezzan, where the population was gentle and good-natured, slaves, treated as members of the family, seldom sought to return to their homes, and in Tripoli too a slave was usually treated with humanity. Even the Awlad Sulayman, brutal and cruel as their general behaviour frequently was, commonly treated their slaves in humane fashion and accepted them into the family circle. Nachtigal quoted several cases of slaves who had no desire whatever to return home. His guide and protector on his journey into Awlad Sulayman country, a man for whom he expressed a high regard, owned one small boy of 13 who steadily refused to be ransomed by his father, a prosperous man who frequently attempted to negotiate his release. Another man, not, strictly speaking, a slave, but an unransomed prisoner of war, highly skilled as a tracker, was given the greatest freedom to practise his expertise, and never showed any sign of wanting to escape. A slave girl, who had an aged relative in the same family under her complete control, was apparently a contented member of the family group.

A recent study of slaves among the Tuareg describes how, through the classificatory kinship system and in particular through avoidance and joking relations, slaves are incorporated into the same social pattern as their masters, and made an integral part not only of the society but also of the actual family. While it is rare for a slave to eat with his master, and slaves live with wind and sun screens rather than in tents, there is otherwise little difference, and clothing and ornaments of free and slave are much the same. This sort of incorporation, of slaves into the slave-owning society, was quite common in Africa. In Hausaland, a slave, if acquired young enough, might be given the tattoo marks of his master's people. In North Africa, a bondman frequently took the name of the tribe of his master. . . . owning society was furthered by special organizations amongst the slaves themselves. In Mecca, each community of Negro slaves had its own shaykh, who settled disputes amongst the members of his community, issuing judicial sentences which were carried out by a supporting official, the *naqib*. In Ghadames, there was but a single shaykh of the slaves. . . . There was also a street of the slaves in Ghadames, where the slaves used to gather and talk.

Evidence of the sometimes comfortable circumstances of slaves comes from various quarters. Here is an East African description:

> No starved and ill-used slaves are to be seen, for on cases of inhumanity being reported to the Sultan [of Zanzibar], the sufferers are at once set free, and made safe from the brutality of their masters. . . .

Parallel instances of the possibility of intervention, should a slave be ill-treated, might be cited. Among the Tuareg a runaway slave may be reclaimed by his owner, but the senior chief may intervene in cases where the slave has been misused or inadequately clothed. According to Muslim law the judicial authority might decree the enfranchisement of a slave whose master had intentionally done anything to him which appreciably diminished his value, or would in the eyes of the world be considered degrading or humiliating, e.g. the amputation of a part of the body or cutting off the hair of a beautiful female.

Slave conditions in general were, however, by no means idyllic, particularly in countries which imposed poverty-stricken limitations upon even the free. The life of a slave in Tibesti was inevitably comfortless and harsh. He was subjected there to "continuous hunger treatment," and his position was particularly hopeless, since the physical conditions of the country made it practically impossible to run away; cases were known where slaves from Bornu had committed suicide. Desert conditions which the Awlad Sulayman accepted as a matter of course placed a very severe strain upon slaves from more fertile countries in the south. Nachtigal was on one occasion astonished to find himself, while on the march, delivering an exhausted slave girl of her newborn infant; the father, presumably a fellow-slave, no one could identify. A poem from Mauritania illustrates what may have been the general opinion about the comforts to which slaves were entitled, though it suggests that in practice these were sometimes enlarged. The poem begins: This world is topsy-turvy but the world to come is sure; and it includes the line:

> The slave is owner of two flowing shifts, while the slave girl keeps her weight through drinking milk.

Under harsh circumstances, an enterprising slave might try to run away. Slave dealers in Ghadames had iron manacles and leg fetters—made, ironically, in the Negro lands—to prevent slaves from escaping, though these were apparently not very much used. Slave caravans coming to Ghadames did occasionally lose runaway slaves, although such fugitives in the desert almost certainly perished. A slave girl in Tibesti, who gave Nachtigal much useful information about her home country, Ennedi, had been eager to escape, even after bearing her master a child. She had, accordingly, for some time been kept in chains, but when she seemed to grow less discontented, the chains were dropped. There was then another attempt to escape, and it was apparently while she was again in chains that she was allowed to have regular talks with Nachtigal, who brought her daily to and from her master's house. Eventually she quarrelled with her master's free wife; being on this account threatened with transfer to another master, she ran away again, breaking her chains, and leaving her small son behind, this time for good. In Bagirmi, two slave women, assigned by Abu Sekkin to Nachtigal, who was having trouble in getting his domestic work performed, also had their feet fastened together with short, heavy chains. They soon ran away, to Nachtigal's secret satisfaction. The propensity of slaves to run away was apparently sufficiently strong in Bagirmi to make the right of one important official to retain all fugitives who were not reclaimed by their masters a valuable perquisite. "Some slaves," said Baba of Karo, "have been with your family so long that they become like your grandmothers," and when slavery was stopped in Hausaland, nothing much happened, so she reported some sixty years later, in her father's slave compound. The fact, however, that "some slaves which we had bought in the market ran away" at that time suggests that not all of them had been perfectly contented with their lot.

The legal texts also took account of the fugitive contingency, in a multitude of incidental provisions: in tax assessment, a runaway slave was counted for some taxation purposes (*zakat al-fitr*), but not—even if the owner hoped to regain him—for others (ordinary *zakat*), and a marriage involving a runaway slave as dowry was invalid.

Even when the ordinary day-to-day life of a slave was tolerable, insecurity continued to be a normal characteristic of the slave condition, for a variety of different, and unpredictable, circumstances might lead suddenly to his or her sale or transfer. A Kanuri, whom market shortages had cut off from his kola nuts, the favourite luxury of Bornu, might, so Nachtigal said, when kola came back into the market, part with his horse or his concubine in order to buy some. A slave who accompanied his master on a journey might find himself left behind in some strange place as payment of some toll-obligation which his master had to meet, or as a contribution to a present to some magnate along the road. Or a slave-owner who fell on hard times might feel that in order to improve his liquidity position he had no alternative to selling some of his slaves. Slaves might be requisitioned as compensation, or as fines. In Vai country, in the seventeenth century, the compensation for adultery with a wife of the king was gifts or slaves. Among one people in the Nassarawa Province of northern Nigeria, if a murderer was caught he was handed over to the family of the victim to be killed; but if the murderer escaped, a male or female slave, depending on the sex of the murdered person, was presented to the bereaved family. In Mauritania, blood-money might include slaves: the loss of an ear was compensated by the gift of a woman slave, while lesser wounds received varying numbers of camels. Slaves forming part of the marriage gift of a fiancé to his intended bride would normally return to his home; but the law allowed the bride's father to sell such slaves, if more money were needed for the trousseau. . . .

Nor did the emancipation of a slave necessarily assure to his descendants unquestioned social acceptance; the taint of slavery in the family genealogical tree sometimes continued to be a liability. Some illustrations of the disabilities from which a member of a distinguished family might suffer if he happened to have a slave as a mother are [frequent], and the tension which has continued in Mauritania between the Negroes whose ancestors were once slaves and other sections of the population [is well known]. In Liberia in 1874 the Negro American traveller, Benjamin Anderson, was told that the Mandingoes of Musadu had such "a hard-hearted and unalterable opinion respecting the freest man if he has once been a slave" that he thought it prudent to cut out from a Monrovia newspaper which he had been given for distribution in the interior of the country a passage which "contained an unsavoury revelation about our once being slaves." In quite recent times a social distinction is said sometimes to remain in marriage alliances, and cases are known of West Africans who had planned a marriage with an American Negro going to the United States for the wedding ceremony to avoid any risk of unpleasantness with their family at home.

The extent to which the slave population reproduced itself is a disputed question on which our authorities have little to say. [Lord] Lugard once asserted that "it is a known fact that slaves do not increase naturally to any appreciable extent," but this so-called demographic law has been categorically rejected by other writers as a "myth." . . .

Special provisions had sometimes to be made for the runaway Muslim slaves of non-Muslim masters, and even of Muslim masters living outside *dar al-Islam*, that is, territory under recognizably Islamic authority. Al-Hajj Umar wrestled with this problem, recommending that a slave who fled to *dar al-Islam* from a Pagan master should become a free man—even if the slave were not a Muslim. Opinions differed, continued al-Hajj Umar, concerning slaves who adopted Islam but did not flee to *dar al-Islam:* some said that these, according to Muslim law, became theoretically free immediately upon conversion, and that this freedom would be extended to them in practical reality should a Muslim army ever invade the Pagan territory in which they lived; but others thought that perhaps the army should take possession of such slaves. If a Pagan slave converted to Islam before his Pagan master, he became free, but not if the master converted first—although some lawyers did argue that a Muslim slave, fleeing from a Muslim master who lived outside *dar al-Islam*, became free on entering *dar al-Islam.* These legal details, painstakingly analysed by scholars, might acquire considerable practical importance in the case of a Muslim reformer waging religious war, endeavouring to extend *dar al-Islam* and to attract as many adherents as possible—and such a man, *par excellence*, was al-Hajj Umar himself.

Occasionally, the fugitive Muslim slave found himself as far outside *dar al-Islam* after his flight as before; but in such case, if he held fast to his religious convictions, he might become the pioneer of Islam in a new area. The first Muslims, for example, to establish themselves in the Eastern Cape in South Africa were runaways from Cape Town, who settled at Uitenhage about 1809.

*part three*

# *REVISING OUR VIEWS*

1

# BRAZILIAN SLAVERY EXAMINED

Was slavery in Brazil less harsh than elsewhere, as Tannenbaum had suggested? Should slavery merely be viewed as an extension of the patriarchalism which one finds, according to Brazil's great historian, Gilberto Freyre, throughout the whole of Brazilian society? Might Brazilian slavery therefore be a microcosm for the nature of social communication within the society as a whole? Or must one view slavery as a series of unique conditions, differing not only from colony to colony or continent to continent but virtually from county to county, from plantation to plantation? In asking the last question, historians of slavery (and of Latin America) were reflecting the trend to be seen in British imperial history as well, toward an atomistic emphasis upon individual responsibility for an annexation, an act of cruelty, or an act of kindness, toward the thesis that the men on the spot, the actual administrators, overseers, and local officials gave imperialism, or slavery, its meaning. Since Brazilian slavery stood at the center of the liberal argument about comparative slave conditions, it was among the first to be examined in local detail. Stanley J. Stein (1920-     ), Professor of History at Princeton University, investigated Vassouras, a Brazilian coffee county, for the last half of the Nineteenth Century. While coffee plantations differed from cotton, and while interior practices—distant from law enforcers—might differ from coastal or island practices, Stein's conclusions, published in 1957, were among the early attacks on the view that slavery had been less harsh within Portuguese-speaking areas.

On isolated fazendas, amid numerous slaves, planters perceived the precariousness of their situation. Many declared openly "The slave is our uncompromising enemy." And the enemy had to be restrained and kept working on schedule through fear of punishment, by vigilance and discipline, by forcing him to sleep in locked quarters, by prohibiting communication with slaves of nearby fazendas, and by removing all arms from his possession. Where fazendeiros judged that one of their number did not maintain adequate firmness toward his slaves, they applied pressure, direct or indirect. Manoel de Azevedo Ramos discovered this when he brought charges against the overseer of a nearby plantation for beating unmercifully one of his slaves. Neighbors testified that Azevedo Ramos enforced little discipline on his establishment, and the case was dropped since witnesses refused to testify in his behalf. To judge by tasks assigned him, the model planter was an omnipotent, omnipresent, beneficent despot, a father to his "flock" of slaves when they were obedient and resigned, a fierce and vengeful lord when transgressed. And, unlike the urban slaveholder whose punishments were somewhat regulated by law, "on the fazendas of the interior the master's will decided and the drivers carried it out." Lightest of punishments might be the threat "Mend your ways or I'll send you to the Cantagallo slave market," more serious might be the age-old instruments of corporal punishment.

Most visible symbol of the master's authority over the slave, the whip enjoyed several names: there was the literate term *chicote* for what was usually a five-tailed and metal-tipped lash, colloquially known as the "codfish" or "armadillo tail." Probably because Portuguese drivers went armed with such cat-o'-nine-tails, slaves tagged it with the name of the favorite article of Portuguese diet—codfish. It . . . was difficult to apply legal restraints to the planters' use of the lash. When one of the founding fathers of Vassouras, Ambrozio de Souza Coutinho, proposed, as one of the municipal regulations of 1829, that "Every master who mistreats his slaves with blows and lashes, with repeated and inhuman punishment proven by verbal testimony . . ." be fined, fellow-planters refused to accept it. Not sheer perversity but the desire to drive slaves to work longer and harder motivated liberal use of the lash. "Many inhuman fazendeiros," wrote Caetano da Fonseca, more than thirty years after Souza Coutinho, "force their slaves with the lash to work beyond physical endurance. These wretched slaves, using up their last drops of energy, end their days in a brief time." And, he added, "with great financial damage to their barbarous masters." Indeed there were masters who believed "their greatest happiness was to be considered skillful administrators, men who force from their slaves the greatest amount of work with the smallest possible expense."

Whipping was not done by the senhor himself who "ordered his overseer to beat the slaves." The whipping over, overseers rubbed on the open wounds a "mixture of pepper, salt and vinegar," probably as a cauterizer but interpreted by slaves as "to make it hurt more." An ingenious labor-saving variation of the whip was reported by ex-slaves. This was a water-driven "codfish" by which a whip secured to a revolving water-wheel lashed slaves tied to a bench. So widespread was use of the lash, that terms such as "fulminating apoplexy" and "cerebral congestion" were employed as medical explanation for death induced by whipping. Typical is an eye-witness account of a beating told by an ex-slave. On orders from the master, two drivers bound and beat a slave while the slave folk stood in line, free folk watching from further back. The slave died that night and his corpse, dumped into a wicker basket, was borne by night to the slave cemetery of the plantation and dropped into a hastily dug grave. "Slaves could not complain to the police, only another fazendeiro could do that," explained the eye-witness.

Only slightly less brutal than the whippings were the hours spent by male and female slaves alike in the *tronco*, a form of heavy iron stock common on plantations. Arms and legs were imprisoned together forcing the victim to sit hunched forward with arms next to ankles, or to lie on one side. This was the *tronco duplo;* the *tronco simples* merely imprisoned legs. One ex-slave claimed that she had been told that the fazendeiro placed her to her mother's breast to nurse while her mother served her punishment in a tronco duplo. Another variation was the long wooden stock (*tronco de pau comprido*) into which were locked the feet of four or five slaves. For inveterate offenders an iron hook or collar (*gancho*) was used to encircle the neck. . . .

As a complement to supervision, to discipline, and to fear of corporal punishment, fazendeiros hoped that the local priest, on visits to plantations of his parish, would use the sermon to "rehabilitate the Negro's condition, to consecrate his relations with his master, who would thereby no longer appear as proprietor or tyrant but rather as father, as a portrait of God, whom he should love and serve with the sacrifice of his toil and sweat." The Barao do Paty suggested that the conscientious confessor instil in the slave "love for work and blind obedience to his masters and to those who control him." Such an attitude other Vassouras planters expressed laconically as "religion is a restraining force and teaches resignation" and therefore planters should "push by every means the development of religious ideas." Planters were not to quibble over the costs of the visiting priest, for "in addition to being necessary for the good, the spiritual grazing of souls, such expenses contribute heavily to maintain the morality, order, submission and proper discipline of . . . slaves who cannot be kept in hand and controlled merely by temporal punishment." Padre Caetano da Fonseca advised that "confession is the antidote of slave insurrections," that the confessor was to teach the slave to see in the master a father and therefore owed him "love, respect and obedience." Through the confessor, explained this priest, the slave learned that "this life is as nothing compared to eternity" and that "the slave who bears his captivity patiently finds recompense in the heavenly kingdom where all are equal before God." . . .

In a society, half free and half slave, many Vassouras planters maintained harmonious relations with the individual members of their labor force. Strong attachments based upon affection and mutual respect often obscured the harsh reality of slavery. A notable difference developed between the affluent planters and the proprietors of small holdings with regard to this relationship. While the large planter had to employ intermediaries to direct the activities of his labor force, the sitianite directed his few field hands personally, resided in unpretentious quarters hardly better than those of his slaves, even "maintained his slaves as part of his family and fed them on the same fare."

It appears, however, that slaves bore perennial animosity toward planters as a group. While slaves in general accommodated themselves to the conditions of their existence, few were ever reconciled to them. Range of reaction was wide—from merely verbal acquiescence to masters' orders to violent, organized insurrection.

To defend themselves against masters trained to "absolute dominion" who were always ready to interpret independent thought as insubordination, slaves responded automatically "Sim-Senhor" to any positive command or opinion and "Nao-Senhor" to the negative. "Slaves never resist outwardly" and . . . where a command demanded no immediate execution, "the slave considers it a law permitting him to do nothing." Mistresses knew they could not order a cook to perform other household tasks. Slave washerwomen or nurses "refuse to wash floors, or they will do so sloppily, soiling walls and curtains; their retort is ready: 'that's not my work.' " Or, in more subtle form of reaction similar to a slowdown in effect, they forced the master "to repeat several times each new detail."

Not always as subtle or restrained was the reaction to a regime where "fear and coercion" were believed the only techniques for obtaining work. Portuguese overseers, as symbols of authority constantly in the view of slaves, suffered much violence. "A slave of the widow, Dona Joaquina, shot Manoel, overseer of the house and land of the widow, and it is necessary that he be severely punished to avoid repetition of similar acts which are extremely poor examples especially in places where the slave population considerably exceeds the free," was reported in Vassouras in 1837. On the Sao Roque plantation a slave who "lost control over his felings when his overseers refused to stop beating his wife, seized a shotgun and shot him." In the last two decades of slavery, attacks on overseers mounted as rumor spread that imprisoned slaves received food and clothing without work. Such ideas could not be extirpated and the local newspaper advised its readers that "there is an erroneous belief that under the penalty of perpetual 'pena de galés', which is almost always imposed for slave crimes, slaves' existence is less harsh than that which they bear under private ownership." When a crime was committed, slaves surrendered voluntarily to the police, confessed the crime "with cynical disdain and tranquilly awaited inevitable condemnation." Thus, Faustino, "slave of Dr. Antonio José Fernandes, killed his overseer with a billhook at 8:30 P.M. and then gave himself up," recorded the same local newspaper which concluded: "Rare is the week when such facts are not registered."

Where slaves could not bring themselves to react by passive resistance or violence, many committed suicide. "Eva, slave of Francisco Soares Torres, a planter of the parish of Mendes, committed suicide on April 7th with a knife blow in the abdomen." Similarly, "on the morning of November 3rd, Maximiano, slave of José Manoel Teixeira Coelho, committed suicide by cutting open his stomach." According to an ex-slave, some slaves hung themselves, "to avoid a beating" and others "to make themselves useless to the master." . . .

Many slaves escaped to the woods until accidentally discovered or rounded up by local police and planters helped by agregados and slaves. Since coffee groves were usually prepared near virgin forest, slaves working in gangs asked permission to leave to attend to physical necessities then fled. Others chose to flee in the dusk as gangs returned from the fields. Others managed to crawl from their locked quarters during the night. As early as 1824 so troublesome were slave flights that planters requested the Câmara Municipal to hire a slave-catcher (*capitao do mato*) to hunt down and recapture fugitives. . . .

In a society where manumitted slaves were common, apprehension of fugitives was not easy. Recapturing fugitives gathered in *quilombos* [organized fugitive communities] was one thing, finding them after they had fled to other coffee growing towns, another. An unknown Negro was likely to be sent to the local jail "on suspicion of being a runaway," inasmuch as manumitted slaves (*libertos* or *forros*) were hard to distinguish from runaways who passed themselves as freedmen and sought employment as rural salaried labor. Masters carried the names of fugitives on their plantation accounts for years in the hope they could someday be recaptured. One inventory listed "Little John, African, forty-nine years old, a fugitive about 10 years" and "Clemente, Brazilian-born, thirty-six years old, a runaway about 6 years." Slave holders placed advertisements in local newspapers describing their runaways with extraordinary care to distinguish them from thousands of others. There were African fugitives: "The slave Mariano, African, has fled from this town. His color is a bit lighter than black, average height, thick beard with bald spots, no front teeth, small eyes, speaks well, dressed in blue cloth blouse and trousers of the same material, madapollam shirt with a worn linen center, cloth cap of military cut. He also wears a black alpaca coat much used, cotton duck trousers, a cotton shirt. Stumbles when he walks because he was locked up in Vassouras' jail for a long time. Wears his cap or hat pulled forward." . . .

. . . It was the haunting fear of mass reaction, insurrection, that terrorized masters and their families throughout the period of slavery. Many could recall the revolting slaves of Manoel Francisco Xavier who formed an organized group more than 300 strong in 1838 and supplied with "all the tools sufficient to form a new fazenda . . . withstood the musket fire" of local police and planters until troops from Rio . . . defeated them. . . . The dramatic impact of this episode brought the adoption of a stringent slave code in the same year, regulating the movement and assembly of slaves and their possession of any arms. These measures failed to inhibit repeated abortive uprisings during the forties, the decade when the largest number of Africans arrived at Vassouras plantations. What one aged resident of Vassouras termed a "zum-zum" or threatened insurrection was noised abroad by slaves in 1848, then quickly squelched by masters who circulated warning letters to neighbors. Mindful of the violent slave revolts in Bahia during the 1830's, Vassouras planters dreaded that among the northern slaves sold southward when African importations ceased, unscrupulous planters would include those who "least suit their owners because of their evil disposition and incorrigible comportment." The commission of Vassouras planters formed in 1854 instructed its members to use every means to convince planters of the "danger of insurrections and of the need to take measures which hinder and prevent so terrible a misfortune as soon as possible." "If the fear of a general insurrection is perhaps still remote, nevertheless the fear of partial uprisings is always imminent, particularly today when our plantations are being supplied with slaves from the North who have always enjoyed an unfortunate reputation. We have had partial insurrections in various spots, and unfortunately they will not be the last." In following years isolated references in municipal archives to group resistance may be largely attributed to the exaggerated fears of planters, to malicious statements by quarreling slaves eager to settle accounts with their fellows, or to incitement by a few slave leaders. Despite planters' fears, Vassouras slaves are reported to have harbored animosity toward the northerners or *Bahianos*, who felt themselves culturally superior. To this element of division among slaves may be added the activity of slaves who curried favor with their masters by offering to help catch fugitives or by informing on their companions. Slaves are reported to have ostracized the slave tale-bearers (*chaleiras*), refusing to speak to them or to aid them in their work. Furthermore, when the chaleira could be enticed from under the overseer's eye, a group of slaves might maul him unmercifully.

Passage of the Rio Branco law (1871), the rising tide of abolitionist sentiment, and discussion of abolition at masters' dinner tables and over the counters of country saloons and stores frequented by slaves, spread among slaves "hopes never before felt, spurring them with the prospect of a smiling future around the corner" and apparently made slavery less tolerable. The worsening situation forced a newspaper of the province of Rio to announce in 1877 that in one town "all planters and their families dread attacks at any moment. In view of the attitude of the slaves their existence and personal security run great risk." . . . There was a permanent undercurrent of insubordination ("refusals to obey, passive disobedience") that slaveholders tolerated to avoid "aggravating the crisis." "The slave no longer obeys or obeys reluctantly, and even runaways are protected by the tacit or avowed complicity of a large segment of the population."

At this point, the problem of mounting slave reaction to forced labor and to the master became more than a matter for local repression. It became the problem of Brazilian labor in general, linked closely to the spread of transportation lines, decline of older coffee plantations, and the rise of an urban middle class. The protest of slaves against their status in a changing society now became part of the nationwide movement for abolition.

2

# THE MYTH OF THE FRIENDLY MASTER

A refutation of the views of Tannenbaum and Elkins was particularly well put by Marvin Harris (1927- ), Professor of Anthropology at Columbia University, and with a pungency welcome if not often seen in scholarship. More recently Franklin W. Knight, in *Slave Society in Cuba during the Nineteenth Century* (Madison, 1970), has subjected Tannenbaum's views to an intensive analysis for a single slave economy and has, as Harris before him, concluded that the notion of a "humane" slavery requires redefinition. The selection that follows is drawn from Harris's influential work of 1964, *Patterns of Race in the Americas* (New York), an early comparative analysis.

The current vogue of opinion about [the] contrast [between Latin America and the British colonies] derives in large measure from the work of Frank Tannenbaum, a noted United States historian, and Gilbero Freyre, Brazil's best known sociologist. The theories of these influential scholars overlap at many points. It is their contention that the laws, values, religious precepts and personalities of the English colonists differed from those of the Iberian colonists. These initial psychological and ideological differences were sufficient to overcome whatever tendency the plantation system may have exerted toward parallel rather than divergent evolution.

Freyre's theories, originally proposed in his classic study of Brazilian plantation life, *Casa grande e senzala,* have remained virtually unchanged for over thirty years. What most impresses Freyre about Brazilian slavery is the alleged easy-going, humanized relations between master and slave, especially between master and female slave. Slaves, while subject to certain disabilities and although sometimes cruelly treated, frequently came to play an emotionally significant role in the intimate life of their white owners. A high rate of miscegenation was one of the hallmarks of this sympathy between the races. The Portuguese not only took Negro and mulatto women as mistresses and concubines, but they sometimes spurned their white wives in order to enjoy the favors of duskier beauties. Behind these favorable omens, visible from the very first days of contact, was a fundamental fact of national character, namely, the Portuguese had no color prejudice. On the contrary, their long experience under Moorish tutelage is said to have prepared them to regard people of darker hue as equals, if not superiors. . . .

Other colonizers were not as successful as the Portuguese because their libidos were more conservative. Especially poorly endowed sexually were the "Anglo-Saxon Protestants." . . .

The next and fatal step in this line of reasoning is to assert that the special psychological equipment of the Portuguese, not only in Brazil but everywhere in "The World the Portuguese Created," yields hybrids and interracial harmony. In 1952, after a tour of Portuguese colonies as an honored guest of the Salazar government, Freyre declared that the Portuguese were surrounded in the Orient, America and Africa with half-caste "luso-populations" and "a sympathy on the part of the native which contrasts with the veiled or open hatred directed toward the other Europeans." . . .

It is true that the Portuguese *in Portugal* tend to be rather neutral on the subject of color differences, if they ever think about such things at all. But this datum can only be significant to those who believe that discrimination is caused by prejudice, when the true relationship is quite the opposite. When the innocent

Portuguese emigrants get to Africa, they find that legally, economically and socially, white men can take advantage of black men, and it doesn't take long for them to join in the act. Within a year after his arrival, the Portuguese learns that blacks are inferior to whites, that the Africans have to be kept in their place, and that they are indolent by nature and have to be forced to work. What we call prejudices are merely the rationalizations which we acquire in order to prove to ourselves that the human beings whom we harm are not worthy of better treatment.

Actually the whole issue of the alleged lack of racial or color prejudice among the Portuguese (and by extension among the Spanish as well) is totally irrelevant to the main question. If, as asserted, the Iberians initially lacked any color prejudice, what light does this shed upon the Brazilian and other Latin American lowland interracial systems? The distinguishing feature of these systems is not that whites have no color prejudices. On the contrary, color prejudice as we have seen is a conspicuous and regular feature in all the plantation areas. The parts of the system which need explaining are the absence of a descent rule; the absence of distinct socially significant racial groups; and the ambiguity of racial identity. In Portuguese Africa none of these features are present. The state rules on who is a native and who is a white and the condition of being a native is hereditary. . . .

As for miscegenation, the supposedly color-blind Portuguese libido had managed by 1950 to produce slightly more than 50,000 officially recognized mixed types in an African population of 10 million after 400 years of contact. This record should be compared with the product of the monochromatic libidos of the Dutch invaders of South Africa—in Freyre's terms Anglo-Saxon Protestants to the hilt—a million and a half official hybrids (coloureds). It is time that grown men stopped talking about racially prejudiced sexuality. In general, when human beings have the power, the opportunity and the need, they will mate with members of the opposite sex regardless of color or the identity of grandfather. Whenever free breeding in a human population is restricted, it is because a larger system of social relations is menaced by such freedom.

This is one of the points about which Tannenbaum and

Freyre disagree. Tannenbaum quite correctly observes that "the process of miscegenation was part of the system of slavery, and not just of Brazilian slavery. . . . The dynamics of race contact and sex interests were stronger than prejudice. . . . This same mingling of the races and classes occurred in the United States. The record is replete with the occurrence, in spite of law, doctrine, and belief. Every traveler in the South before the Civil War comments on the widespread miscegenation. . . ." But it should also be pointed out that there is no concrete evidence to indicate that the rank and file of English colonists were initially any more or less prejudiced than the Latins. It is true that the English colonists very early enacted laws intended to prevent marriage between white women and Negro men and between white men and Negro women. Far from indicating a heritage of anti-Negro prejudices, however, these laws confirm the presence of strong attraction between the males and females of both races. The need for legal restriction certainly suggests that miscegenation was not at all odious to many of the English colonists.

The idea of assigning differential statuses to white indentured servants and Negro workers was definitely not a significant part of the ideological baggage brought over by the earliest colonists, at least not to an extent demonstrably greater than among the Latin colonists. It is true, as Carl Degler has shown, that the differentiation between white indentured servants and Negro indentured servants had become conspicuous before the middle of the seventeenth century even though the legal formulation was not completed until the end of the century. But who would want to suggest that there was absolutely no prejudice against the Negroes immediately after contact? Ethnocentrism is a universal feature of inter-group relations and obviously both the English and the Iberians were prejudiced against foreigners, white and black. The facts of life in the New World were such, however, that Negroes, being the most defenseless of all the immigrant groups, were discriminated against and exploited more than any others. Thus the Negroes were not enslaved because the British colonists specifically despised dark-skinned people and regarded them alone as properly suited to slavery; the Negroes came to be the object of the virulent prejudices because they and they alone could be enslaved. Judging from the very nasty treatment suffered by white indentured servants, it was obviously not sentiment which prevented the Virginia planters from enslaving their fellow Englishmen. They undoubtedly would have done so had they been able to get away with it. But such a policy was out of the question as long as there was a King and a Parliament in England.

The absence of preconceived notions about what ought to be the treatment of enslaved peoples forms a central theme in Tannenbaum's explanation of United States race relations. According to Tannenbaum, since the English had gotten rid of slavery long before the Discovery, they had no body of laws or traditions which regulated and humanized the slave status. Why this legal lacuna should have been significant for the course run by slavery in the United States is quite obscure. Even Degler, who accepts the Freyre-Tannenbaum approach, points out that it was "possible for almost any kind of status to be worked out." One might reasonably conclude that the first settlers were not overly concerned with race differences, and that they might have remained that way (as many Englishmen have) had they not been brought into contact with Negroes under conditions wholly dictated by the implacable demands of a noxious and "peculiar" institution.

Let us turn now to the main substance of Tannebaum's theory. Tannenbaum correctly believes that the critical difference between race relations in the United States and in Latin America resides in the physical and psychological (he says "moral") separation of the Negro from the rest of society. "In spite of his adaptability, his willingness, and his competence, in spite of his complete identification with the *mores* of the United States, he is excluded and denied. . . ." Also, quite correctly, Tannenbaum stresses the critical role of the free Negro and mulatto in Latin America. Manumission appears to have been much more common, and the position of the freed man was much more secure than elsewhere. Free Negroes and mulattoes quickly came to outnumber the slaves. However, according to Tannenbaum, this phenomenon came about because the slave was endowed with "a moral personality before emancipation . . . which . . . made the transition from slavery to freedom easy and his incorporation into the free community natural." The Negro and mulatto were never sharply cut off from the rest of society because the Latin slave was never cut off from the rest of humanity. This was because slavery in southern Europe and Latin America was embedded in a legal, ethical, moral and religious matrix which conspired to preserve the slave's individual integrity as the possessor of an immortal human soul. The "definition" of the slave as merely an unfortunate human being, primarily according to state and canonical code, is given most weight. . . . Note that it is not merely being claimed that there was a critical difference between Latin American and United States race relations during and after slavery, but that the very institution of slavery itself was one thing in the United States and the British West Indies and another thing in Latin America. . . .

The contention that the condition of the average slave in the English colonies was worse than that of the average slave in the Latin colonies obscures the main task which confronts us, which is to explain why the treatment of the free mulatto and free Negro were and are so different. To try to explain why the slaves were treated better in Latin America than in the United States is a waste of time, for there is no conceivable way in which we can now be certain that they were indeed treated better in one place than the other. It is true that a large number of travelers can be cited, especially from the nineteenth century, who were convinced that the slaves were happier under Spanish and Portuguese masters than under United States masters. But there was plenty of dissenting opinion. Tannenbaum makes no provision for the fact that the English planters had what we would today call a very bad press, since thousands of intellectuals among their own countrymen were in the vanguard of the abolitionist movement. The West Indian and Southern planters, of course, were in total disagreement with those who preferred slavery under foreign masters. Actually all of the distinctions betwen the Anglo-American and Latin slave systems which Tannenbaum proposes were already the subject of debate at the beginning of the eighteenth century between Anglo-American abolitionists and Anglo-American planters. . . . All slave-owners of whatever nationality always seem to have been convinced that "their" slaves were the happiest of earthly beings. . . .

If one were so inclined by lack of an understanding of the nature of sociological evidence, it would not be difficult to paint a picture in which the position of the Anglo-American slave system was promoted from last to first place. . . .

. . . Better to dispute the number of angels on a pinhead than to argue that one country's slavery is superior to another's. The slaves, wherever they were, didn't like it; they killed themselves and they killed their masters; over and over again they risked being torn apart by hounds and the most despicable tortures in order to escape the life to which they were condemned. It is a well known fact that Brazil was second to none in the number of its fugitive slaves and its slave revolts. In the seventeenth century one successful group held out in the famous *quilombo* of Palmares for sixty-seven years and in the nineteenth century scarcely a year went by without an actual or intended revolt.

In a recent book, the historian Stanley M. Elkins attempts to save Tannenbaum's theory by admitting that slavery in the United States (at least by 1850) "in a 'physical' sense was in general, probably, quite mild" and that there were very "severe" sides to the Spanish and Portuguese systems. Elkins assures us, however, that even if slavery had been milder here than anywhere else in the Western Hemisphere, "it would still be missing the point to make the comparison in terms of physical comfort. In one case we would be dealing with cruelty of man to man, and, in the other, with the care, maintenance, and indulgence of men toward creatures who were legally and morally *not* men—not in the sense that Christendom had traditionally defined man's nature." It is devoutly to be hoped that Elkins shall never be able to test his exquisite sense of equity by experiencing first thirty lashes dealt out by someone who calls him a black man and then a second thirty from someone who calls him a black devil. . . . [W]e had better take a closer look at the proposition that the Negro was regarded as a human being by the Latin colonists but not by the Anglo-Saxons. The principal source of evidence for this resides in the law codes by which the respective slave systems were theoretically regulated. Admittedly, these codes do show a considerable difference of legal opinion as to the definition of a slave. The Spanish and Portuguese codes were essentially continuations of medieval regulations stretching back ultimately to Roman law. The British and American colonial codes were the original creations of the New World planter class, developed first in the West Indies (Barbados) and then copied throughout the South. Although the Constitution of the United States said that slaves were persons, state laws said they were chattels—mere property. . . . On the other hand, Spanish and Portuguese slave laws did, as Tannenbaum claims, specifically preserve the human identity of the slave: "The distinction between slavery and freedom is a product of accident and misfortune, and the free man might have been a slave." From this there flowed a number of rights, of which Fernando Ortiz identifies four as most significant: (1) the right to marry freely; (2) the right to seek out another master if any were too severe; (3) the right of owning property; and (4) the right to buy freedom.* Tannenbaum shows how all of the U.S. slave states denied these rights. He goes further and shows how the U.S. slaves were virtually left without legal remedy for harms committed upon them, and he emphasizes the casual fines which protected the life of a slave under the early laws, and the total lack of legal recognition given to the slave's affinal or consanguine family. Indeed, for every favorable section in the Spanish law, both Elkins and Tannenbaum readily find an unfavorable section in the Anglo-Saxon codes.

What the laws of the Spanish and Portuguese kings had to do with the attitudes and values of the Spanish and Portuguese planters, however, baffles one's imagination. The Crown could publish all the laws it wanted, but in the lowlands, sugar was king. If there were any Portuguese or Spanish planters who were aware of their legal obligations toward the slaves, it would require systematic misreading of colonialism, past and present, to suppose that these laws psychologically represented anything more than

---

* *Los negros esclavos* (Havana, 1916), p. 303.

the flatus of a pack of ill-informed Colonel Blimps who didn't even know what a proper cane field looked like. Ortiz leaves no room for doubt in the case of Cuba. Yes, the slave had legal rights, "But these rights were not viable . . . if they contrast with the barbaric laws of the French and above all, of the English colonies, it was no less certain that all of these rights were illusory, especially in earlier times. . . ." Sanctity of the family? "Man and wife were permanently separated, sold in separate places, and separated from their children." "How many times was a son sold by his father!" and "Pregnant or nursing slaves were sold with or without their actual or future offspring." Protection of the law? "The sugar and coffee plantations were in fact feudal domains where the only authority recognized was that of the master. . . . Could the Negroes hope in these circumstances to change masters? The rawhide would quiet their voices. . . ." Rights to property? "From what I have said in relation to the work of the rural slave, to speak of his right to hold property and to buy freedom, is futile. . . ." "But I repeat, the plantation slave was treated like a beast, like a being to whom human character was denied. . . ."

Tannenbaum makes much of the fact that there was no set of ancient slave laws to which the Anglo-Saxon planters or the slaves could turn for guidance. He prominently displays the meager penalties attached to murder of slaves as examples of their sub-human status in the eyes of the Anglo-Saxon colonists. But Ortiz informs us that "it was not until 1842 that there was any specific legal regulation of the form of punishment which a Cuban master could give his slave." Actually it turns out that "the state did not concern itself with the limitation of the arbitrary power of the master in relation to the punishment of his slave until after the abolition of slavery [1880]."

In Brazil, as everywhere in the colonial world, law and reality bore an equally small resemblance to each other. Stanley Stein's recent historical study of slavery in the county of Vassouras during the last century yields a picture almost totally at variance with that drawn by Gilberto Freyre for the earlier plantations. The Vassouras planters went about their business, methodically buying, working, beating and selling their slaves, in whatever fashion yielded the most coffee with the least expense. The master's will was supreme. . . . The Brazilian slave owners were convinced that Negroes were descended from Cain, black and "therefore not people like ourselves." Making due allowance for exceptions and the special circumstances of household slaves [Charles] Boxer concludes that "it remains true that by and large colonial Brazil was indeed a 'hell for blacks.' "

# 3

# CARIBBEAN RACE RELATIONS

There were two forms, or variants, in race relations in the Caribbean, arising from two overlapping but different facets of daily life. The tension between the realities arising from the day-to-day relationships and those held to by a people as a part of their ethos would produce what Harmannus Hoetink (1931-    ), a Dutch scholar at the Netherlands School of Economics in Rotterdam, would see as an ironical guilt complex. Hoetink's work, *De gespleton samenleving in het Caribisch gebied*, published in Holland in 1962, would become well known in America after its publication, as translated into English by Eva M. Hooykaa in 1967, as

The relations between members of different races in a society must be divided into two categories. The first category concerns the non-intimate relations between the races in superficial, everyday intercourse. These relations form part of the social atmosphere, the *ambiance*, in which people live together: the rules of behavior which regulate the inter-personal but non-intimate contact between groups.

In this category the influences of . . . European cultural variants, . . . are certainly extremely significant. It is in this sphere that positive differences between the Iberian and North-West European variants can be observed. . . .

The everyday contact between members of heterogeneous groups in Iberian society is undoubtedly marked by social suppleness, by an apparently spontaneous (albeit often artificial and superficial) warmth, which finds its physical expression in the *abrazo* and other physical expressions of social contact. All this can be said to flow from a sophisticated and well-developed technique for creating the requisite atmosphere for such contacts in a socially, economically, and racially divided society, where objectively speaking many points of friction exist between the various groups. The latent conflict is not reduced, but is so completely submerged by this deluge of uninhibited mutual friendliness that it is apparently checked, at least during the temporary contact, and the reflex show of friendliness is hardly recognized as artificial.

It seems likely that the long-standing and frequent contacts of Iberians with alien cultures have promoted this social suppleness. It seems equally likely that, on the North-West Europeans' side, the influence of Protestantism is noticeable in the degree of inhibition in social contacts, in the imposed, forced friendliness which seems to be the most a Calvinist can produce (speaking generally and to point the contrast), in the coldness and awkwardness which characterize his superficial contacts even in the mother country, and, *a fortiori*, in a society containing numerous "alien" groups.

I am prepared, therefore, to accept Tannenbaum's threefold division of the Caribbean, though not in his terms—of the relative cruelty of their slave systems—but rather in those of social skill in everyday intercourse with other races and cultures: the Iberians at one end and the North-West Europeans at the other end of the scale (with the Dutch probably at the extreme end within this group?), and the French in the centre.

The other category of race relations concerns the willingness of the members of the different races to enter into intimate personal relations based on social equality; this category is characterized by willingness to enter into sexual relations, incurring social acceptance, with a member of a different racial group. This second category implies biological-cum-social mingling of the races; that is, marriage in the sociological sense, as opposed to those forms of miscegenation based on incidental or permanent relations as may exist between master and slave, white and non-white, in which the social cleavage is always preserved. It is the intimate personal interracial contacts which ultimately determines the fate of a racially segmented society: whether it will become a single *people*, in the sense of a cultural group whose members' feeling of belonging in the last instance is based on common descent.[1]

The relations described in the first category have no direct influence on social stratification, for the slave remains "slave," the Negro "Negro," and the white "white," whatever the nature of their personal relations. The rate at which relations of the second category occur, on the other hand, determines the structural dynamism of mixed societies. . . .

Tannenbaum considers that the degree of liberality or cruelty in systems of slavery is determined mainly by the favourable or unfavourable influence of religion and law in a society. . . . He rightly states that, however important the legal provisions with regard to the slave were in Spanish and Portuguese areas, in the long run they were less decisive than the prevailing "social arrangements and expectancies" and thus subordinates formal laws and the juridical concept of the slave to the actual practice of social reality. Tannenbaum apparently considers that this subordination applies only to the Latin American area. As soon as he begins to discuss the situation in the south of the United States, he regards the law as more decisive: "the many thousands of instances of kindness, affection and understanding between master and slave . . . these were personal and with no standing in the law. Legally there was no effective remedy against abuse and no channel to freedom."

Tannenbaum may be criticized not only for this inconsistency but also for his assertion that there was no legal protection for slaves in the southern United States. There was the "Black Code" of Louisiana of 1806, not quite two decades after the famous Spanish American Code. The Louisiana Code stipulated that, generally, slaves should not be made to work on Sundays; if they did, they had to be paid for their labour. It also prescribed in detail the minimum in food and clothing to which slaves were entitled, and the treatment of sick slaves. It stated that half an hour should be allowed for the morning meal and one and a half hours for that in the afternoon; that disabled slaves might not against their wish be sold without their children, and that children below the age of ten should not be sold separately from their mothers. The Code also laid it down that anybody might lodge a complaint with the court on behalf of a maltreated slave. Justices of the Peace were empowered to obtain information regarding the maltreatment of slaves in their district and to institute legal proceedings when this occurred.

On the other hand, Tannenbaum's enthusiasm for the Brazilian slave laws might be somewhat diminished by the arguments by the contemporary Brazilian scholar Florestan Fernandes. The latter demonstrates that the *Codigo Negro* was not linked to the Constitution, nor to the civil code, and the position of the slave in Brazil was, in fact, marked by his complete *incapacidade civil.* He himself had no right to lodge a complaint with the court, but could do this only through his master or another free citizen; he could not bear witness against his master; he could, in the public interest, be used as an informant, but could not be a sworn witness.[2]

There is no need to mention or analyse further the official directives regarding the treatment of slaves in the Caribbean, for the social reality of the application of these protective laws is far more significant than the laws as such. It is in this respect that Tannenbaum merits most criticism, for he did not sufficiently appreciate the extent to which this reality was affected by economic factors. . . .

. . . Tannenbaum not only extends the supposedly greater liberality of slavery in Spanish America to the essentially different sphere of race relations, but also tends to regard evidence about the social position of Brazilian coloureds as valid also in respect of the Brazilian free Negro. He tends to identify the two groups, and in his book the word "Negro" is used most frequently, while he uses "mulatto" only incidentally, to add force to his argument: that "the Negro, especially the mulatto" occupied a more favourable position in Brazil than in the United States. For Tannenbaum, then, the mulatto is a special kind of Negro. Thus, Tannenbaum applies the North American concept of "Negro" to the Brazilian situation: that is to say that North American standards (by which anyone who is known to have a certain amount of Negro "blood" in his veins is regarded as a Negro and treated accordingly by the white man) are applied in the evaluation of a society in which wholly different standards were (and are) valid, and where the distinction between Negro and coloured had (and has) considerable social significance. . . . It seems curiously paradoxical that an investigator like Tannebaum, whose moral concern about the race problem in his own country is evident from his publications, finds it so difficult to detach himself from the standards of his own society and applies them uncritically to other societies.

Tannenbaum is not the only North American whose evaluation of the race problem in other societies is clouded by this conceptual self-delusion. Cahnman remarked, with reference to [Donald] Pierson's *Negroes in Brazil*, that this book "stands for a type of literature on South America which is most revealing if read between the lines. It reveals that the main practical difference between Anglo-American and Latin-American race-attitudes is in the position of the Mulatto rather than the Negro." [3] Indeed, this fusion of the two concepts "Negro" and "coloured" into one, "Negro," which is then, incidentally, analysed into its special components, makes it necessary to read between the lines in order to achieve any real distinction between the Latin and North-West European variants. . . .

. . . It is paradoxical that, whereas formerly reproaches were aimed at the systems of values, views, opinions of "exotic" cultures, now they are aimed at those of one's own civilization, with the implication that the investigator then appears to regard himself as more objective. The previous reproaches arose from the absolute acceptance of one's own system of values; today's self-reproach comes from the absolute acceptance of one's own "fall." I fail to understand why self-reproach is less inimical to objective evaluation than are the reproaches of others. These self-reproaches in the Western world (the world of the mother countries) are the expression of feelings of guilt which are closely connected with one's own *Zeitgeist* (or awareness of downward movement) as soon as this manifests itself as a special form of group subjectivity in relation to the other *Zeitgeist* (or awareness of upward movement).

NOTES

1. P. J. Bouman, *Sociologie, begrippen en problemen* (Antwerp, 1947), p. 73.
2. R. Bastide and F. Fernandes, *Relações Raciais entre Negroes e Brancos em Sao Paolo* (Sao Paolo), 1955, p. 77. The conclusion of these authors regarding the lack of status of the Brazilian slave is also reached by Octavio Ianni in his *As Metamorfoses do Escravo: Apogeu e Crise da Escravatura no Brasil Meridional* (Sao Paulo), 1962. Ianni also stresses the limitations in the judicial position of the freed slave in Brazil.
3. W. J. Cahnman, "The Mediterranean and Caribbean Regions: A Comparison in Race and Culture Contacts," *Social Forces*, XXII (May 1944), 210, n. 5.

4

# ABSENTEE OWNERSHIP IN THE WEST INDIES

Slavery also had a profound effect upon white society. In the West Indies it would contribute to the decline of the sugar estates and to the general instability of society in a variety of ways. Some of these ways are examined by a West Indian scholar who teaches at the University of the West Indies in Mona, Jamaica, Orlando Patterson (1936- ), in his book *The Sociology of Slavery*.

The basic and dominating element in Jamaican slave society was that of absenteeism. This element was central to the whole social order and was in some way related to almost every other aspect of the society. So central was it indeed, and so much was it the root of all the evils of the system, that we may describe the white Jamaican community as an absentee society. A rigorous distinction must be drawn between structural causes and consequences of absenteeism and its historical causes, the reason being that once absenteeism had fully emerged it consolidated itself, and its own evil effects were the very causes of its continuation. . . .

Those few Jamaicans of the early period who were of the British upper-middle class were the first to return home, having restored their fortunes. As the century progressed the early settlers who had monopolized most of the land and had made their fortunes began sending their children to England to be educated and few of them returned. By the middle of the eighteenth century 300 children a year were leaving Jamaica for England. The system of primogeniture also led to an increase in absenteeism. Younger children were often provided for by annuities charged against the estate. These children never had any first hand connection with the source of their income and cared even less about it. When, as so often happened, a younger brother inherited from his deceased elder kin, the estate came to be owned by someone who had never seen his property and had little intention of doing so.

We derive a very good estimate of the extent of absenteeism and the degree to which inheritance worsened the situation, by analysing an abstract of wills relating to Jamaican estates between 1625 and 1792. Of the 307 wills actually abstracted (312 are listed but five are missing) 142 of the testators were resident in England at the time they made their wills, while only 133 were resident in Jamaica. Interestingly, fifty two of the 142 English-based testators were residing in London, while the second largest group from a single area came from Bristol. Fourteen of the testators made their wills just before going to Jamaica: one of these claimed that he was formerly of Jamaica and now residing in England but "shortly bound back" for Jamaica. . . . Of those residing in England, thirty claimed that they were "formerly of Jamaica" but "now residing in England." Between 1625 and 1750 there were twenty one such testators. In the last forty two years of the period of the wills there was a rapid proportional increase, nineteen of the testators "formerly of Jamaica" now residing in England. On the other hand, only four persons were residing in Jamaica who were formerly of England before 1750 and only one such after 1750. This certainly indicates the large numbers who left Jamaica for England in relation to the few who made the opposite voyage.

It seems as if almost all widows of Jamaican husbands left for England soon after their husband's death. All seven of the testators who were widows and residing in England at the time of making their wills claimed that they were "formerly of Jamaica" during the lifetime of their spouse. Of the rest of the wills, one testator was "bound shortly for England" from Jamaica; two were resident in Ireland; one in France; five were either in the Army or Navy and the residence of nine was not made clear by the abstracts.

Even more revealing are the contents of these wills. The Jamaican estates went, in almost every case, to relatives in England. One can easily imagine that these inheritors, having no intimate link with the islands and perhaps unwilling to give up their particular course of life, would gladly settle for an attorney in the island to supervise his or her estate, thus adding to the number of absentee owners. . . .

By the nineteenth century, when the plantation system began to collapse, a large number of indebted estates were foreclosed upon by English creditors who had no interest whatever in residing in the island. An observer, writing 16 years after the abolition of slavery, claimed that the foreclosure of mortgages led to an even greater number of absentee owners, so that nine-tenths of all the land under cultivation in the island before emancipation was owned by absentees.

It is reasonable to conclude therefore, that since about the middle of the eighteenth century, while the majority of land and slave owners may have been resident, the distribution of the slaves and other property of the island was skewed so heavily in favour of a few wealthy proprietors, most of whom resided in England, that most of the slaves and property can be said to have been owned by absentee landlords.

Let us now consider the consequences of absenteeism for Jamaica. Its most striking effect was the fact that the island was drained of the very people it needed for leadership in all aspects of life. From the beginning to the very end of slavery, the governors of the island frequently wrote to Whitehall complaining that they were unable to find suitable men to fill the council and other important offices. In 1696, for example, Lieutenant Governor [Sir William] Beeston was so short of qualified men that one of the Councillors, who had been expelled from his position because of treasonable association with the French, had to be reinstated, the Governor explaining to the Lords that "there are not men enough of parts and integrity left in the country to discharge those greater trusts." Often Beeston could not even get the required quorum of seven members, since the incompentent few who were necessary to make up the quorum often chose deliberately to hold up the processes of government by refusing to answer their summonses.

One hundred and thirty-eight years later, during the apprenticeship period, the Marquis of Sligo, who was then Governor, wrote of the Council that they were:

> a sad set indeed with some exceptions. Several have been put in merely for the protection of their persons being overwhelmed with debt . . . would that I could find an opportunity of getting rid of them. . . . Their poverty and inefficiency is a matter of public notoriety, they have no influence, they enjoy no respect, and reduce the character of the body to such a degree that it is hardly considered of the legislature at all.

. . . Absenteeism was also the cause of the gross lack of proper education in the island. The leaders of the white community viewed the matter of establishing schools with utter contempt. . . . Although several large donations had been made toward the building of schools, few of them found fruition. The occupation of teacher was "looked upon as contemptible, and no Gentleman keeps company with one of that character." A few wealthy planters sent their children to be educated in England, but the majority remained semi-literate and were the common butt of every conversation. This lack of education and the complacency of the leading planters in regard to it, was, in turn, one of the main factors intensifying absenteeism. . . . Most of the children of the wealthy planters sent to England to be educated never returned. . . .

The absence of the most educated and civilized members of the society also led to a complete breakdown of religion and morality among the resident whites since the local leaders were among the most profligate people imaginable. What was worse, the clergymen themselves were often among the most immoral in the island and the established Anglican church in Jamaica represents, perhaps, the most disgraceful episode in the history of that institution. . . . An article in the *Jamaica Magazine* of July, 1813 commented on the lamentable state of religion in the island, the greater part of the blame being placed on the clergymen who were described as "selfish and mercenary" and condemned their "cold indifference" to the moral state of the island. It was well known that unsuccessful overseers with the right contacts could procure a living as a clergyman. The Reverend David King observed that "Holy orders were readily given to men who were imperfectly educated and of indifferent moral character" and another minister, himself the son of a Jamaican planter, bemoaned the fact that "the clerical office in Jamaica was a sort of dernier resort to men who had not succeeded in other professions."

A very interesting explanation of the laxity in morals, which supports our view that absenteeism was central to most of the evils of the society, is given by Thomas Jelly who makes the important observation that the white population had a high mortality rate leading to a high turnover, most of the new recruits coming from Britain. This, he asserts, was "productive of many evils." First, men seeking a quick fortune could hardly be expected to concern themselves very much with the moral state of a society to which they felt little commitment; and secondly, "the continued influx of strangers" tended "to prevent anything like settled habits of morality or order." [1]

This lack of religion and moral sanctions was partly responsible for a fourth characteristic of the Jamaican white community: the almost complete breakdown of the institutions of marriage and the family. This breakdown was also in part the result of the fact that there were so few women available. One of the most striking features of Jamaican slave society was "the almost total absence of female society." The few available white women were usually the daughters of the small élite of the wealthy resident planters and were accessible only to other members of the creole élite. One can easily sympathize with the disillusionment of a young Scottish book-keeper who complained bitterly of his "forlorn situation" in which he was "utterly debarred from the society of the decent and the virtues of the other sex." Not that the few available white women were all that desirable. As we have already noted, few of the educated women returned. Those who were not educated in England usually received a poor private education by tutors specially hired for the purpose. The general picture one gathers of these women is . . . that they had "much of the quashee," an implication that they were little more enlightened than their slaves. Lady Nugent frequently had cause to bemoan their imbecility, entering on one occasion in her Journal that "Mrs C is a perfect Creole, says little, and drawls out that little, and has not an idea beyond her pen."

But the scarcity of white women was only one of many reasons accounting for the lack of marriage and the family. On most estates in the island marriage was forbidden to the white employees, few attorneys being disposed to employ a man with such an encumbrance. While marriage was proscribed, promiscuity with black or coloured women was positively sanctioned. Henry Coor, a millwright and slave owner in the island between 1759 and 1774 said that, "It was the greatest disgrace for a white man not to cohabit with some woman or other."

The sexual exploitation of female slaves by white men was the most disgraceful and iniquitous aspect of Jamaican slave society. Rape and the seduction of infant slaves; the ravishing of the common law wives of the male slaves under threat of punishment, and outright sadism often involving the most heinous forms of sexual torture were the order of the day. It was common practice for a white man visiting a plantation to be offered a slave girl for the night. [J. B.] Moreton tells us that many of the white employees on the estate had a rotation system whereby they seduced every desirable female on the plantation over and over again. He also informs us of the practice of many of the attorneys who made a grand annual tour of the estates under their supervision with a large retinue of friends remaining at each estate for a number of days during which there were indescribable scences of debauchery, the female slaves being primed in advance of their coming.[2] . . .

But perhaps the most disastrous consequences of absenteeism were to be found in the gross mismanagement of the economic affairs of the ilsland. As early as 1707 the friend of an absentee owner wrote to him describing the hopeless mismanagement of his estates where "all things" were "in disorder, the whole works a pot of nastiness and in general out of repair." . . . The result was that the maangement of the estate was left almost entirely to the overseers who, being paid on a commission basis, forced the slaves to work far beyond their strength and generally depleted the capital of the estate in order to procure high annual returns . . . :

> No attention is paid to fences, to the clearing of pasture lands, or to the repairs of the buildings. Large cane fields are planted without manure; weeds are seen luxuriating in the midst of the canes as they grow up and all classes, old and young, are out at work, under the scourge of the lash, from four in the morning until after dark at night.[3]

At this rate, we are further informed, in eight years the entire capital outlay of the estate is depleted. . . .

But the people who suffered most from the neglect and inefficient management due to absenteeism were, of course, the slaves —whether we view them from the point of view of capital equipment or as suffering human beings. Captain Thomas Wilson said that "It was generally understood where Planters resided themselves, their Slaves were better taken care of than under the direction of Overseers. . . . And Henry Coor further informed the Select Committee that:

> It was more the object of the overseers to work the Slaves out, and trust for supplies from Africa; because I have heard many of the overseers says, "I have made my employer 23, 30 or 40 more hogsheads per year than any of my predecessors ever did; and though I have killed 30 or 40 Negroes per year more, yet the produce had been more than adequate to that loss."

Nor could the slave, as Coor further remarked, expect any relief from the attorney since the latter, too, had a vested interest in exploiting the assets of the owner to its fullest, being paid on a commission basis. Several of the governors of the island attributed the frequent slave revolts of the island to the ill-use resulting from absenteeism and the Jamaican Assembly in an address to the Crown in 1750, expressed much the same view. . . .

## NOTES

1. Thomas Jelly, *Remarks on the Condition of the Whites and Free Coloured Inhabitants of Jamaica* (London, 1826), p. 8.
2. *West India Customs and Manners* . . . (London, 1793), pp. 77-78 [note corrected].
3. B. Mahon, *Jamaica Plantership*, pp. 143-44 [note incomplete in original].

5

# A MARXIST VIEW OF BLACK LABOR

Slavery also contributed to a change in the work habits of Blacks. Under voluntary conditions, or the forms of involuntary servitude found in Africa, they had worked well and helped give rise to complex cultures; in the New World, they worked far less effectively. Some of the reasons for this change are explored by Eugene Genovese (1930-     ), a Marxist scholar who is Professor of History at the University of Rochester and whose work on the political economy of slavery has been widely praised. Most recently he has published a series of Marxist essays, *In Red and Black* (New York, 1970).

Kenneth M. Stampp's *The Peculiar Institution* (New York, 1957) challenges effectively the traditional view that enslavement in America raised the Negro from savagery to civilization. Drawing upon anthropological data, he shows that Africans brought to the United States as slaves had been removed from societies far more advanced than most of our historians have appreciated. Unfortunately, he pays only passing attention to that aspect of the traditional view bearing most directly on the economics of slavery in general and the productivity of black labor in particular.

The Negro slave worked badly, according to some leading historians, not because he was a slave but because he was a Negro.

This argument has taken two forms: (1) the Negro has certain unfortunate biological traits, such as a migratory instinct or an easygoing indolence; and (2) the Negro came from a lower culture in Africa and had to be disciplined to labor. The first argument does not require refutation here; the negative findings of genetics and anthropology are conclusive and well known. The second argument raises serious economic and social questions. In the words of Lewis C. Gray:

> The great body of Negroes came to America ignorant savages. Care was requisite to prevent them from injuring themselves with the implements employed. It was necessary to teach them the simplest operations with hand tools and to instruct them in the elementary methods of living—how to cook, put on their clothing and care for their houses. . . . Under competent supervision the Negro acquired peculiar skills in picking and hoeing cotton and other simple routine operations of field labor.[1]

Ulrich B. Phillips defends slavery as a historically progressive institution that assembled the working population in a more productive pattern than had existed previously. He then implies that enslavement in America civilized the Negro and disciplined him to labor. Probably, ancient slavery often did play the role Phillips suggests, but to accept that generaliation by no means commits one to the corollary drawn for American Negro slavery. Phillips gives no evidence but refers to the views of the sociologist Gabriel Tarde, who, we are told, "elaborated" on Thomas R. Dew's idea that enslavement domesticated men much as animals had been domesticated previously.[2]

An examination of Tarde's discussion shows that it offers little support to Phillips. The idea of reducing men to slavery, Tarde suggests, probably arose after the successful domestication of animals, and in both cases the subjected were tamed, transformed into beasts of burden, and made productive for others. Tarde's ideas should be considered within the context of his theory of imitation, according to which an enslaved people learns from its conquerors, whereas the latter do not deign to absorb the ways of their victims. This idea is in itself dubious—how much richer is Hegel's analysis of "Lordship and Bondage" in his *Phenomenology of Mind*, in which the interaction of master and slave is so brilliantly explored—but if it has any relevance to the problem at hand, it merely suggests that the Negro in America came into contact with a higher culture. Who, outside the ranks of the most dogmatic cultural relativists, would argue with such a generalization? On the central question of labor productivity. Tarde's thesis is valid only if we assume that the Negro had to be brought to America to acquire the habit of systematic agricultural labor. Phillips never puts the matter quite that baldly, but his analysis rests on this proposition.

Phillips' interpretation of African life has had a profound effect upon students of American Negro slavery, but it depends on the now discredited work of Joseph Alexander Tillinghast and Jerome Dowd. According to Tillinghast, African Negroes were "savages," subject to the "unfathomable . . . mysterious force" of heredity. The West African population before the European conquest supposedly had no cereals and survived on a bare subsistence of vegetable roots. Tillinghast, Dowd, and others upon whose work Phillips draws have applied untenable methods, made dubious assumptions, and produced work that anthropologists today consider of little or no value.[3] One might be inclined to pardon Phillips and those who have followed him for trusting the judgment of anthropologists were it not that the arguments contain hopeless contradictions, and were it not that even during the nineteenth century some scholars were perceptive enough to warn that anthropologists and other social scientists often fell victim to the racial prejudices permeating European and American life. . . .

The first contradiction in the Tillinghast-Phillips interpretation is the fact of importation, for if the African had not been disciplined to agricultural labor why was he brought here at all? The "domestication" of savages is no easy matter, and only a small percentage of the enslaved usually survive. Europeans first brought Negroes from Africa because they were accustomed to agricultural labor, whereas many of the previously enslaved Indians were not and tended to collapse under the pressure.

Second, in order to show that Africans were backward, Tillinghast and Phillips say that slavery was common among them. And so it was! There is no better proof that African society had "domesticated" its own population before the white man volunteered to assume responsibility. West African peoples like the Ashanti and Dahomey had, in addition to successful labor systems, elaborate military structures, legal arrangements, and commercial relations. A re-examination of the economic structure of West Africa and of its implications for American slavery is therefore in order.

There are other objections to Phillips' argument. He assumes that the Negro, once brought here, retained many African traits, which hampered his productivity. So prominent an anthropologist as Melville J. Herskovits, who certainly does not share Phillips' biases or general conclusions, attempts to prove that the Negro has preserved a large part of his African heritage to the present day. This contention has come under heavy and successful fire from E. Franklin Frazier, who shows that Herskovits' evidence illuminates Brazilian rather than North American experience. American Negroes had contempt for newly imported Africans and set out to "Americanize" them forthwith. As Frazier says, the array of isolated instances of African survivals only indicates how thoroughly American slavery wiped out African social organization, habits, and ways of thought. If we are to avoid baseless racist and mystical assumptions, we shall have to know just what traits the Negro supposedly brought from Africa and kept for generations and just how they affected his productivity. . . . We must conclude, therefore, that the assertion of special traits does nothing more than to restate the original notion of a Negro undisciplined to agricultural labor until brought here.

Phillips has to assume that the poor work habits of slaves amounted to mere negligence or even stupidity, but they often reflected an awareness of economic value and penchant for sabotage. Side by side with ordinary loafing and mindless labor went deliberate wastefulness, slowdowns, feigned illnesses, self-inflicted injuries, and the well-known abuse of livestock and equipment, which itself probably arose within a complex psychological framework. Viewed as such, Phillips' easy notion of ignorant savages making a mess of things falls to the ground.

Most Negroes brought from Africa to North America doubtless came from the West Coast. The Dahomey, famous as slave raiders, rarely went more than two hundred miles inland, and most of their victims lived much closer to the coast. The West African peoples undoubtedly had mature systems of agriculture. The Dahomey even had a plantation system; all these peoples—Dahomey, Ashanti, Yoruba, to mention a few of the outstanding—had significant division of labor. They carried on and carefully regulated a system of trade; craft guilds existed widely; and a class structure had begun to emerge.

The Yoruba, Nupe, and Fulani had absorbed Moslem culture, and when the Fulani overran northern Nigeria, they carried Moslem scholars with them. Before the Fulani conquest, the Nupe of Nigeria had developed an urban civilization partly under Moslem influence. This influence undoubtedly had a positive effect on Negro technical and economic life, but most of the indigenous peoples did not need outsiders to teach them the fundamentals of agrarian life. "West African societies," writes the outstanding authority on Islam in Africa, "had already achieved fully developed techniques and economic organization before Islam made its appearance. Its influence was most evident in the commercial sphere which in the Sudan belt was wholly taken over by Moslems." [4]

The development of mining provides some clues to the economic level of West Africa. Gold and iron mining flourished at least as early as the fourteenth century, and the Arabs drew upon the area for gold. The tales of wonderful metals and metalwork attracted the Portuguese and led to their initial explorations. The peoples of Ghana and Nigeria used iron hoes and other agricultural implements, and the Yoruba of southern Nigeria enjoyed a reputation for fine work in copper and tin. . . .

In contrast to Tillinghast's picture of indolent, berry-picking natives, the proverbs, aphorisms, and customs of the West African peoples indicate that they were accustomed to hard work. Sayings included: "Poverty is the elder of laziness"; "He who stays in bed when he is able to work will have to get up when he cannot"; and "Dust on the feet is better than dust on the behind." Prestige accrued to those who worked hard, fast, and well and was therefore a powerful motivating force. These facts, now taken for granted by anthropologists, are not so surprising when one considers that even in the most primitive societies there is hard work to do. One works, as Herskovits says, because everyone works, because one must work to live, and because it is the tradition to work. The Dahomey, who were among the more advanced of the African peoples, had a reputation for industriousness, held hard work praiseworthy, and practiced crop rotation and agricultural diversification.

The most puzzling aspect of Phillips' position is his awareness of slavery among the West Africans. He remarks that slavery was "generally prevalent" and adds that, according to Mungo Park [a Scottish explorer], the slaves in the Niger Valley outnumbered the free men by three to one at the end of the eighteenth century. Phillips never seems to realize that the existence of African slavery shatters his insistence that the Negroes had not been habituated to agricultural labor. Tillinghast and Dowd, for their part, set the bad example, for in the same books in which they assure us that the Negroes were the laziest of food gatherers they announce that these same Negroes had slaves, debt peons, and private property.

The Dahomey had large crown-owned plantations worked by slave gangs under the direction of overseers whose business was to maximize output. Debt peonage was a well-established institution. Among the Nupe, slaves did a great deal of agricultural labor and reportedly numbered in the thousands by the time of the British conquest. The more primitive tribes of northern Nigeria had been conquered and enslaved by the Nupe before the beginning of the nineteenth century. The Ashanti had an elaborate system of family land ownership and imposed a light *corvée* on those of low status. The tribes of the Ashanti hinterland practiced slavery, debt peonage, and systematic agriculture. The Ashanti defeated one of these tribes, the Dagomba, at the end of the seventeenth century and obligated it to produce two thousand slaves annually. The Ibo of southeastern Nigeria, slave traders as well as a source of slaves, produced several important crops with servile labor. During the eighteenth and early nineteenth centuries the great West African peoples—the Yoruba, Dahomey, and Fulani—fought continually for control of southwestern Nigeria, and each in turn enslaved thousands during the wars.

African slavery was far removed from New World slavery in many respects and perhaps ought not to be considered under the same rubric. The Ashanti economy in which slaves participated strove, for example, toward autarky. The system of land tenure placed a brake on individual accumulation of land, and status therefore rested primarily on political and social rather than economic criteria. However surprisingly, masters had no power over the economic surplus produced by their slaves, who worked for themselves. . . . The term "slavery" applied to West African societies could easily mislead us, for the slaves held therein functioned in the economy without special disadvantage. Apart from the gloomy possibility of ritual execution, the worst a slave suffered was to have to endure as a pariah who could be shifted from one household to another by sale. Since no mechanism for economic exploitation existed, no impassable barriers to freedom did either. The ease with which a slave might be adopted into the family as a free man varied markedly in time and place but remained noticeable. Because of certain peculiarities of property inheritance in a matrilineal society, there were even special advantages in taking a slave for a wife. Two conclusions emerge: West Africans had disciplined themselves to agricultural labor; and the transfer of a slave from an African to a European master meant a profound change in the nature and extent of his obligations.

The absence of slavery, in any form, among some of the coastal peoples does not imply that agriculture was undeveloped or that hard work was lacking. The Bobo, for example, who were probably an important source of slaves for the United States, refused to hold slaves but had a reputation for being conscientious laborers.

Angola and the Congo supplied numerous slaves to South America and some to North America. These peoples, too, came from societies resting on agricultural foundations. The Bantu-speaking peoples of southwestern Africa practiced slavery, although to what extent we do not know. The more primitive and undeveloped peoples, including some cannibals, did not supply slaves from among their own but did act as slave catchers for the Europeans.

For a general statement of the economic level of pre-colonial West Africa we may turn to the distinguished former premier of Senegal, whose credentials as a student of African history and culture are not in question. Writes Mamadou Dia in his essay on "L'Économie africaine avant l'intervention européenne":

> The traditional African economy does not deserve to be treated disdainfully as a primitive economy, based on static structures, with technical routines incapable of adapting themselves to new situations. Everything proves, on the contrary, that this agricultural economy showed evidence of a strong vitality with possibilities for creating or assimilating techniques appropriate to assure its survival.[5]

The African economy was nevertheless much less developed than that of the European world, and we may assume that the productivity of the Negro was well below that of the white man of Western Europe. We need not rush to accept the grotesque exaggerations about the level of West African society that currently are flooding the literature. Emancipation would not have suddenly accomplished the miracle of raising the productivity of the Southern Negro to the level of, say, the Northern farmer. Since the Negro was accustomed to agricultural work in Africa as well as in the South, the task of raising his productivity should not have been difficult. In a friendly society, with adequate incentives, the Negro laborer's efficiency should have improved quickly. There is no scientific basis for any other assumption.

That the Negro worked hard in African agriculture does not prove that his economic faculties did not decline once he was separated from his homeland. Frank Wesley Pitman writes that Negroes taken to the West Indies knew how to tend their own gardens and care for livestock but were totally unprepared for the work expected of them in the sugar fields.[6] By what process, it may be wondered, does a man prepare himself to be driven in a slave gang? Yet we know that even the slave plantation was known in Africa, and Herskovits has shown that American slavery represented a distorted continuation of the various forms of collective labor common to Africa.

The brutality of American slavery confronted the African—even the African who had been a slave in his homeland—with something new. Under its mildest forms Southern slavery had to be much harsher than its African counterpart. With the partial exception of the Dahomey, African slavery was patriarchal. Even slaves from a conquered tribe were sometimes assimilated into the new culture. A slave might buy his freedom and become a free man in a new homeland. There was little racial antipathy, although it was by no means unknown. In the South the Negro received a series of hard blows. He worked under more stringent conditions, was torn from his culture, family life, and system of values, and found himself in a society that offered no adequate substitutes. If the Negro was "culturally" unattuned to hard work, this condition reflected not his African background but a deterioration from it.

To say that the Negro suffered from a cultural dislocation that may have affected his economic propensities is not to imply that, after all, the Negro slave proved a poor worker because he was a Negro. Enslavement itself, especially the enslavement of a people regarded as racially inferior and unassimilable, produces such dislocations. Once slavery passes from its mild, patriarchal stage, the laborer is regarded less and less as a human being and more and more as a beast of burden, particularly when he is a foreigner who can be treated as a biological inferior. Even in patriarchal societies, slavery facilitates the growth of large-scale production, which corrodes the older comradeship between master and slave. The existence of slavery lays the basis for such a development, especially where markets are opened and institutional barriers to commercialization removed. Such a course may not be inevitable, but slavery does establish a powerful tendency toward large-scale exploitation of men and resources. The rise of the plantation system in Dahomey serves as an illustration, although the economic structure was unusual and cannot be regarded as a mature, commercially oriented slave system. Thus slavery, no matter how patriarchal at first, will, if permitted to grow naturally, break out of its modest bounds and produce an economy that will rip the laborer from his culture and yet not provide him with a genuine replacement.

Even if we judge the problem of the slave South to have been the presence of a culturally dislocated labor force, we should not be justified in asserting that the difficulty lay with the Negro as a Negro. Rather, the cause of the process of dislocation and the deterioration of his work habits was slavery itself. Slavery, once it becomes a large-scale enterprise, reverses its earlier contribution to the productivity of the laborer and undermines the culture, dignity, efficiency, and even the manhood of the enslaved worker.

NOTES

1. *History of Agriculture in the Southern United States to 1860* (Washington, 1933), I, 467.
2. Phillips, *American Negro Slavery* (New York, 1918), p. 344 and n. 1; generally Chaps. I and XVIII; Gabriel Tarde, *The Laws of Imitation*, tr. Elsie Clews Parsons (New York, 1903), pp. 278 f, also p. 221 and *passim.*
3. Joseph Alexander Tillinghast, *The Negro in Africa and America* ("Publications of the American Economic Association," 3rd Series, III, No. 2; New York, 1902), pp. 2 f, 18 f; *cf.* Jerome Dowd, *The Negro Races* (New York, 1907), Vol. I. For a thorough and convincing critique of these works see Melville J. Herskovits, *The Myth of the Negro Past* (New York, 1941), Chaps. I and II, esp. pp. 55-61.

4. J. Spencer Trimingham, *Islam in West Africa* (Oxford, 1959), p. 185.
5. Mamadou Dia, *Réflexions sur l'économie de l'Afrique noire* (nouv. ed.; Paris, 1960), p. 23.
6. "Slavery on the British West India Plantations in the Eighteenth Century," *The Journal of Negro History*, XI (Oct., 1926), 594.

*part four*

# *THE PROBLEM OF INVOLUNTARY SERVITUDE*

1

# SLAVERY AMONG THE INDIANS OF NORTH AMERICA

Slavery is a practice. In time it also came to be a legal condition. Still, the practice had preceded the legal definitions. Scholars have been too inclined, perhaps, to accept the legal definitions and to ignore other, quasi- or extra-legal, forms of slavery, or of involuntary servitude for a term rather than for life. The Indians of North America, for example, held slaves: the Iroquois, the Indians of the Southwest, those of the Northwest Coast of what would become Canada and the United States. Europeans also held Indians as slaves, and in New France the majority of slaves were *panis*. These aspects of slavery have received much less attention than has Negro slavery. In the 1930's a young Russian student, Iulila Pavlovna Averkieva, studying at Columbia University, investigated the nature of slavery among the Northwest Coastal Indians, and in 1935 she presented her findings as a thesis to the U.S.S.R. Academy of Sciences. Translated into English in 1957, her material is of interest at two levels: for its factual (indeed, too factual, for too lacking in interpretation) statement of the many ways in which slaves might be used, giving rise again to the question, must slavery represent a mass or gang labor situation? and for the way it draws upon legend as historically valid evidence.

Slave labour was widely used in conjunction with the labour of tribesmen. A person who enjoyed the use of several fishing weirs needed a large number of workmen for the construction and operation of them. . . . In the main, . . . division of labour . . . was weakly developed, its limits being defined by the mere increase in [the number of members in] the family and the extension of its labour force by way of the inclusion of slaves in its aggregate. . . .

. . . [T]he slaves of the Nootka Indians every now and then were forced to undertake heavy tasks; they acted not only as servants, providing water, wood, etc., but were obliged to build boats, to aid in the construction and the repair of houses, to provide their masters with fish, to accompany them to war and to fight for them. The women were occupied chiefly in the preparation of clothing, in cooking food, in collecting berries, etc. "Among the duties of slaves," . . . writes [a contemporary], "were included the cleaning of salmon, the collection of berries, the carrying of water and wood, and the execution of anything that they were told to do." These are quite substantial services, for the cleaning of fish in the large quantities in which they were taken was an important task; just as essential was the utilization of slaves in the work of collection, for the products of it were not only an important element in their own food supply and that of their masters, but were produced for the market as well. . . .

. . . The circumstance that, side by side with a fantastic element, the conditions of life are depicted quite realistically in the folklore of the tribes [of the northwest coast of North America] affords the possibility of viewing as quite authentic the information in the legends and myths about the economic activities of slaves.

We shall begin with the legends which provide evidence about the utilization of slaves in a basic branch of the economy of the population—in fishing. In one legend of the Haida there is recounted the story of a chief's son who had been abandoned by his father and by the whole tribe and who, while flying in the guise of a gull, saw in a boat his father's slaves catching fish. We find the same theme in Tsimshian myths; in these the chief's son sees his father's boat, in the stern of which sits a female slave and her husband and other slaves are catching fish with a net. Very likely the main theme of this tale—the abandoned son of a chief, with the help of totem animals, obtains food and the tribe which abandoned him starves—crops up independently in each tribe because of the similar conditions of social life. This information about slaves fishing may be considered reliable since it does not contradict the conditions of life of either tribe and is confirmed by other legends. In another legend of the Haida it is recounted that a slave of a chief was not only an excellent hunter but had also a special chest for his fishing equipment, which he took with him always. In the Kwakiutl legend "About the Salmon" a slave goes to the salmon weir for fish. Almost all these tales depict slaves as persons who catch fish independently. Neverthless they were often used as a subordinate labour force and the role of director of the fishing belonged to their masters who themselves participated in the fishing. Among these same Haida, in an account of a war with the Tlingit, it is recounted that a Tlingit was at a fishing site with his wife and two slaves, one of whom was killing the salmon with stones. We meet also a whole series of references to hunting by slaves; for example, in the Kwakiutl legend about "Weight-on-Floor" there is mention of a slave hunting with the son of a chief. In another legend of the same tribe it is reported that "A chief, Hamalak'ana'e, sent 10 slaves to hunt seals." "Hex'hak'in sent several slaves to hunt seals; the slaves brought back 50 seals." In one of the Haida legends slaves set out on a hunting expedition with the chief's nephew; in another legend of the same tribe the chief's slave was a good hunter and had a magic spear for sea-otters.

As in fishing, slaves hunt alone and also with their masters. When the catch or the proceeds of the hunt are brought back the slaves unload it and drag it to the house of the chief. In berry picking, however, female slaves always work with the daughters or the wives of the chiefs. In one of the Tsimshian legends the chief's wife goes with slaves to gather berries; in another legend it is recounted that "a codfish was the slave of a supernatural being and collected wild berries for it." In a Tlingit tale about the origin of copper we read that the daughter of a chief sets out with female slaves to collect berries. In the Kwakiutl legend about

"Oldest-One-in-the-World" we read that "Many-Coloured Woman," a chief's daughter, "had 12 slaves with whom she set out to collect wild rice, and the slaves served not only as collectors of rice but as oarsmen." Slaves are depicted as oarsmen in the majority of legends in which they are mentioned.

There is frequent mention of slaves serving as fellers of trees and carriers of wood and water. In the Kwakiutl legend about "Killing-at-North-End-of-World," a slave goes for wood. In another legend of this same tribe there is depicted the slave of a salmon who, using wooden wedges, cuts down trees and then drags them from the water's edge to the house. In a Haida legend there is mention of four village slaves who come for logs to the sandy shore of an inlet. In one of the Tsimshian legends the son-in-law of a chief plans [to go] to the forest for wood, but the father-in-law, since he owns many slaves, will not permit him to do that. Usually such work is done by the sons-in-law, nephews and other relatives of a chief, but in this legend the chief, in order to emphasize his wealth, forbids his son-in-law to cut wood.

There is very little indication of the use of slaves in the making of canoes. But in the Kwakiutl legend about "Copper-Maker" the chief orders his forty slaves to construct a canoe and in one of the Haida legends slaves are sent to take care of the canoe. Probably slaves were seldom used for such a task since it required certain skill[s] which, as a rule, slaves did not possess.

Slaves assist the chief's son to prepare arrow-tips. In one of the Kwakiutl legends there is an account of a slave who dives for shells and who, with the chief's son, makes arrow [-tips] from them. All the dirty work around the house was done by slaves. In one of the Haida legends we read that "in the house there was so much human excrement that the slaves had to carry it out in buckets." Slaves lay the fire in the house of the chief and are sent to the neighbouring village or neighbouring house for live coals.

In a Kwakiutl legend "a person by the name of 'Red-Morning Sky' told his servants, his sweeper and procurer of fire, to make all things ready. The fire-maker immediately laid the fire and the sweeper swept the house." Later on two sweepers came and swept the right side of the house. Then 4 servants served food. Slaves prepare food and serve their master and his guests. "Chief-of-the-World," in Kwakiutl legends, orders his slave to bring clover roots and to cook them. The slaves secured the roots and placed them on hot stones; they were transformed into snakes and the guests recoiled from such a repast. Then the chief ordered the slave to go to the salmon weir and see whether or not there were fish in it; the slave immediately went there and quickly returned with two salmon which he roasted and set before the guests. In another legend an old woman, the slave of a chief, asked the guests to sit down; the chief ordered her to feed his son's women. The chief "Echo," in a Tsimshian legend, orders his slave to roast a dried salmon. Slaves spread mats and valuable furs for their masters and for guests. . . .

The daughters and wives of chiefs were always accompanied by female slaves. In one of the Haida legends the following is recounted: "Women looked after the chief's daughter. . . ." In another legend of this same tribe it is reported that the daughter of a chief had ten female slaves. Her parents attempted to give a slave, instead of their daughter, in marriage. "The two women sang; their voices were very beautiful; soon they arrived at his place. They were both very beautiful." He thought that they were two sisters but then it was disclosed that one was a chief's daughter and the other was her slave. The appearance of the daughter of one of the Haida chiefs is described [thus]: "She came with a throng of female slaves." In one of the Tsimshian legends female slaves accompany the wife of the chief everywhere and the chief questions them about the conduct of his wife. In Tlingit legends the daughter of a chief takes with her a female slave and his son a slave. A chief's son almost always has a slave of the same age as himself, who in childhood plays with him and when the son reaches manhood the slave accompanies him everywhere. . . . There were frequent instances of close friendship between master and slave. A slave accompanies his master on hunting trips and on expeditions where he usually serves as bearer of arms and rower; during the trip he makes the fire and prepares the food for his master. . . .

Old, infirm slaves looked after the children. In Kwakiutl legends we read, "The wife of the chief issued the command, 'Come here, you who rock this crying child.' Presently there appeared 40 old men. 20 sat down on the left side of the cradle and 20 on the right; two took hold of the right side of the cradle and two, the left. . . . The figures here are evidently an exaggeration but are important evidence of the fact that for this work old slaves, unsuitable for other work, are used. In the same source, we find, in another instance, evidence which testifies to the use of slaves for the same purpose; a father, turning to his son, says, "These forty slaves and forty-sea-otter skins will go to you." These forty slaves were to be used for rocking a crying child. In Tsimshian legends a chief orders his slaves to carry about a child who is crying. In the same legends a female slave trains the son of a chief and slaves look after him, prepare for him pitch for chewing, and take him every day to an island where he likes to play. The wife of a chief orders her slaves to prepare ample food for her son; the slaves feed him but nevertheless he still is hungry. . . .

# 2

# SLAVERY IN AFRICA

As elsewhere in antiquity, there was slavery in Africa. As elsewhere in the world, men sold their own kind into slavery, for the slave trade could not have existed without the middlemen, themselves black Africans. These simple statements of fact have recently taken on intolerable burdens of propaganda: look, see, say many whites to the blacks who demand Freedom Now, your ancestors were enslaved by your own people, not by our ancestors alone; the guilt for slavery falls equally upon your hands as upon ours. Look, see, say many blacks, how thoroughly the European demand for labor could corrupt a pre-industrial society. Yet, as Basil Davidson (1914- ), a London-based journalist and historian of Africa, shows in the selection that follows, while there was slavery in Africa, it was to be compared functionally more to European feudalism than to New World slave systems, Servitude would take on many different guises.

It would be an illusion to see the feudalism of Africa as being the same as the feudalism of Europe in these opening years of discovery. But the similarities were often strikingly close. They are worth dwelling on because nothing but powerful feudal organization can properly explain the military strength of many

African states that were found by Europe in the fifteenth and sixteenth centuries, and respected by Europe (at any rate in the beginning) as allies and partners and equals.

To get at the true position, one must look at the nature of society as it had evolved in the maturity of Africa's Iron Age. A useful approach, especially in the light of what was to come, is from the standpoint of who was bond and who was free. In Western Europe during the Dark Ages, the formative period of feudalism, there had come a gradual transformation of slave into serf; and this change was accelerated in feudal times until "old slave" and "old freeman" were little by little merged together into "new vassal." In Africa, meanwhile, wherever strong states and empires shook and changed the old framework of tribal equality, there emerged the new phenomenon of mass subjugation of one people by another. This was not slavery as Europe understood the word—chattel slavery, the stripping from a man of all his rights and property—but serfdom, vassalship, "domestic slavery." Degrees of servility and obligation would immensely vary with time and place, as they would elsewhere; but this vassalship in Africa would become essentially the same as that of Europe. . . .

Not much more than a hundred years ago the little army of Amadou Hammadi, founder of the Fulani empire in the Macina grasslands of the Middle Niger, faced their much more powerful assailants in a battle for survival. They took the field in doubt and great anxiety. Amadou gave the command of his army to his henchman Usman and bestowed on him the title of Amirou Mangal, "great chief." Then tradition makes Amadou say to Usman: "Great chief, raise your eyes and look about you and tell me what signs you see." Amirou Mangal does as he is bidden and replies: "Verily, I see on every hand the signs of our victory. I see that God is with us." At this point there enters the herald of the "invincible" king of Segu. He rides up with his entourage in a grand flurry of horses and banners and demands that Amadou Hammadi should at once surrender, admit homage to the king of Segu, pay tribute, and be gone. "For otherwise the vultures shall tear your flesh."

Calm of heart, Amadou answers with a mocking smile and says to the herald: "A messenger can meet no evil. Be welcome here, bold herald, and you shall have refreshment." As for submitting to the king of Segu, "let him know that my submission is already to God and will be made to no man."

That is one example among many, and completely African. Yet King Henry V before the Battle of Agincourt said nothing different to the herald of King Louis of France, although he may have said it, thanks to Shakespeare, somewhat better:

> There's for thy labour, Mountjoy.
> Go, bid thy master well advise himself:
> If we may pass, we will; if we be hinder'd,
> We shall your tawny ground with your red blood
> Discolour; and so, Mountjoy, fare you well.

The medieval states of the Western Sudan repeatedly show how closely the condition of subjugated peoples—commonly referred to, alike by Arabs and Europeans, as "slaves"—resembled that of feudal vassals. In the Songhay Kingdom of the fifteenth century along the Middle Niger, "slaves" from the non-Muslim peoples of the forest verge were extensively used in agriculture. They were settled on the land and tied to it. In return for this livelihood they paid tribute to their masters both in crops and in personal services. Their bondage was relative: time and custom gave them new liberties. Yet being generally restricted by feudal rule in the varieties of work they might undertake and the peoples among whom they might seek wives, these "slaves" tended to form occupational castes. They became blacksmiths, boat-builders, stablemen, makers of songs, bodyguards of their sovereign lord. Along with the "free peasants," whose social condition was really little different, these "vassal peasants" and "vassal artisans" formed the great bulk of the population.

Contrasts in status between the freeman who belonged to a conquering people and the "slave" who came of a conquered people would grow narrower as time went by and the system grew stronger; and in this too, there was a broad parallel with medieval Europe. Caste and even class divisions might emerge and sharpen among the mass of "commoners"; the dominant factor in society increasingly became the difference in power which separated prince and lords from the people, from all the people. This stratification occurred among the strong nations of the forest belt, behind the coast, just as it appeared among the Muslim peoples of the northern plains. It was narrowly limited by the nature of West Africa's feudal economy which remained largely one of subsistence and barter. It was greatly modified by the electoral principle of chiefdom and the checks and balances of customary rule. But the lord-and-vassal stratification nonetheless grew sharper among the groups who held power. There are many examples.

Early in the nineteenth century the old Hausa states of northern Nigeria were taken over by an invading army of Fulani. All the captains and leaders under Usman dan Fodio, the great Fulani leader, were then endowed with large landholdings seized from the defeated Hausa lords (except where these, as occasionally happened, had thrown in their lot with the new regime). The old Hausa royal title of *Sarki* was perpetuated, and the whole titular structure was bound directly to the newly created fiefs and regions of command. And this oligarchy came with time to exercise rights of life and death over the common people, and could call on them for labor in the fields or the building of houses or the maintenance of roads and river fords.

The case is especially instructive, since the origins of this Fulani invasion had lain in revolt against a gross social inequality. Explaining "the reasons for our holy war with the Hausa Sultans," a contemporary Fulani document, written some four years before Europe heard news of the Battle of Waterloo, says that in the beginning Usman dan Fodio "did not address himself to the kings. After a time his people grew and became famous, till they were known in Hausaland as '*The People*.' Men kept leaving their countries and coming to them. Of the ruling classes some repented"—for Usman preached a puritanical Islam, calling on the rich to abandon their wealth and calling on the poor to put their trust in God—"and came to him with all they possessed, leaving their [Hausa] Sultans. Then the Sultans became angry, till there ensued between them and their chiefs the war we remember."

Yet in freeing the people of the Hausa states from their old bondage, the Fulani reformers soon found themselves binding on a new one. However egalitarian Usman dan Fodio might be, his henchmen were ambitious men whose reforming zeal was tempered by a healthy territorial ambition. Besides, they were rulers of their time. They soon found they must either forfeit their new-found power and wealth or else revert to those very methods of bureaucratic government that they had set themselves to overthrow. And little by little, there being in any event no alternative but abdication, the new Fulani feudalism came to resemble the old Hausa system; except for a tightening of Islamic discipline, little was altered but the men at the top. . . .

. . . In nineteenth century Bornu, heir to the ancient state of Kanem in the region of Lake Chad, custom generally recognized three social groups beneath the noble families: the *kambe*, who were freemen drawn from the ranks of freed slaves and the children of freemen married to slaves; the *kalia*, who were slaves, whether foreigners or men and women captured in war; and the *zusanna*, the descendants of slaves, who were also the rank-and-file footsloggers of the army of Bornu. Yet the differences between the *kambe* and the *kalia* and the *zusanna* were undoubtedly less important, so far as the distribution of social power was concerned, than the differences between all these three on one hand and the nobles on the other. Here, once again, was a system recognizably feudal—a system, moreover, which had grown with Iron Age development from the earliest beginnings of the old pastoral empire of Kanem, forerunner of Bornu, during a period that was contemporary with the growth of European feudalism.

Such systems continued into modern times. One other example may be useful from another part of Africa, the kingdom of Ruanda, lying in a small country of tall mountains between the Congo and the East African lands of Uganda and Tanganyika. Ruanda possessed a close-knit social order that persists in large measure even today, so that anthropologists have been able to make direct reports about it.

This society is divided into three kinds of people. Foremost are the Watutsi—of late years much photographed for their splendid dancing—who may number about one-tenth of the population. They, says [J. J.] Maquet, "do no manual work and have leisure to cultivate eloquence, poetry, refined manners." Beneath them are the Bahutu, who "do not enjoy such gracious living," because "they have to produce for themselves and for the Watutsi." And beneath the Bahutu, in the third rank, are the Batwa—"so low social in the hierarchy and . . . considered so irresponsible, that they have had a greater independence of action."

In Ruanda, accordingly, nobody is "free" in the modern sense of the word, for even the Wattusi are wedded to their laborers by a formal code of interwoven duties. Moreover, it is better for a Mututsi (that is to say, one Watutsi) to become the vassal of a strong man than to remain on his own. "We desire," Maquet's Watutsi informants told him, "to become the vassals of great chiefs, or even of the king, because we are then under the protection of somebody very important, we get more cows, and that allows us to have more 'clients' "—that is, more Bahutu workers who will labor in their turn so as to gain "protection."

Compare this "ladder of duty-and-obligation" with that of feudal Europe. Many European slaves were liberated—"manumitted" in the language of the times—but few were then able or desired to remain on their own. They found it better and safer to bind themselves to a master, and they chose the most powerful lord they could find. "The manumitter," [Marc] Bloch has written of medieval France, "even if he agreed to give up a slave, wished to conserve a dependent. The manumitted himself, not daring to live without a protector, thus found the protection he desired." In Europe as in Africa, like causes produce like effects. . . .

Europeans of a somewhat later day often misunderstood the essentially vassal nature of this African subjection. Such slavery, argued the defenders of the slave trade, was no different from any other. This argument they used repeatedly in their eighteenth century battles against those who wished to abolish the trade. Do not prevent us from taking these poor savages away from Africa, the slavers urged, for otherwise you will condemn them to a fate much worse. Confirm us in our right to carry them off to America, and you will encourage "a great accession of happiness to Africa." The British Privy Council of Enquiry into the slave trade, which sat in 1788, was doubtfully impressed. One may note that other men would afterwards urge a continuance of the colonial system with much the same argument. Do not ask us to abandon our responsibilities for governing Africans, for you must otherwise confirm these peoples in a savage fate. . . . Support us in our powers of dominion, and you will ensure rich benefits for Africa. . . .

Set this highly mobile social order alongside the slave system of the United States, and the vital and enormous difference becomes immediately clear. There the slaves were entirely a class apart, labeled by their color, doomed to accept an absolute servitude; in Tannenbaum's words, "the mere fact of being a Negro was presumptive of a slave status." And slave status was forever. . . .

This is not to suggest that the life of an African vassal was one of unalloyed bliss, but that the condition he suffered was in no way the same as plantation or mining slavery in the Americas. His condition often was comparable to that of the bulk of the men and women in Western Europe throughout medieval times. In this respect Africa and Europe, at the beginning of their connection, traded and met as equals. And it was this acceptance of equality, based on the strength and flexibility of feudal systems of state organization, that long continued to govern relations between Africa and Europe. Even in the matter of slaving their attitudes were much the same.

# 3

# SLAVERY IN THE STRAITS SETTLEMENTS

As noted earlier, scholars too often have associated slavery with Africa and the New World, with White over Black, in their attempts to understand the economic and social nature of involuntary servitude. An earlier selection described the nature of debt bondage among Malay sultans, demonstrating that slavery by any other name still remains Slavery. The following essay examines the approach to debt bondage, which they readily identified as slavery, by the British after their accession to power in the Straits Settlements and the Malay States, especially between 1819 and 1920. During this time the British ruled the Settlements—Singapore, Penang, and Labuan—directly, while authority within the States was exercised through the rôle of the resident Adviser, a British civil servant appointed to aid the Malay sultan in all matters not pertaining to succession or the Islamic religion. As this selection makes clear, even within the relatively constricted area of the mainland Malay Peninsula, slavery took on a variety of forms, differing from Pahang to Selangor to the Negri Sembilan, for example. The author, Philip Loh Fook Seng (1940-     ), is on the faculty of the University of Singapore.

Towards the end of the eighteenth century England's "national guilt," the West Indies slave trade and slavery, was very much in the minds of Englishmen, amongst them Granville Sharp, Rev. James Ramsay and William Wilberforce. Sharp, in 1772, successfully prosecuted a slave-owner for detaining a fugitive slave called Somerset on shipboard in English waters. Chief Justice Mansfield ruled that "the black must be discharged," a ruling which had the effect of emancipating 14,000 other black men brought home by retired West Indian planters. They were now legally free, or rather, they had always been free on English soil, a decision (an English historian records) which destroyed "property worth more than half a million pounds." In 1784 Ramsay issued the first of his outspoken pamphlets on the evils of the slave trade. Wilberforce "transformed by an Evangelical conversion," soon afterwards discovered his vocation. So it was with [Stamford] Raffles who, in 1818 at Bencoolen, solemnly presented certificates of freedom to some three hundred slaves owned by the Company, his first act to implement the "principles on which my future government would be conducted," for which he earned the company's reprimand. At a more personal level Raffles bore not only the burden of the white man but a father's loss of his three oldest children between July 1821 and January 1822. The fire was yet to come. Raffles sought solace in his political child, Singapore, to which he came expectant and with "new life and vigour" arriving on 10 October 1822. This was to be his last visit and one of his last acts in Sangapore was the issue of Regulation V for the prevention of the slave trade and the emancipation of slaves.

The immediate cause for the issue of Regulation V of 1823 was Farquhar's *laissez faire* attitude towards slavery and the slave trade. Raffles was generally dissatisfied with his handling of affairs in Singapore, a dissatisfaction made more acute when he discovered that slaves were being landed and sold in Singapore. One dealer "was so confident that he could land and sell his slaves with impunity that he sent Raffles as well as Farquhar one or two slaves as presents."

Farquhar, with his eyes on trade in a young colony like Singapore, was not inclined to be Evangelical, nor was Raffles free from the needs of trade and diplomacy. He was realist enough to make two exceptions—the personal establishments of the Sultan and the Temenggong and the domestic establishments of Native Chiefs or traders in transit were exempted from the regulation "to prevent annoyance or obstruction to the trade of the port." Slaves and slave debtors enslaved before 26 February 1819 were to be declared free only after a period of three years or less, to enable them to "render personal services to their present masters" in payment for "the expense of their passage hither . . . the only legal demand that can be admitted." All other persons who "may have been imported, transferred or sold as slaves or slave debtors, since 26 February 1819" were freed immediately.

The principles governing British policy in the emancipation of slaves in the Native States were initial recognition of native custom in order not to disturb unduly native sensibility; recognition of property including the ownership of persons before British rule, with its corollary of compensation; an immediate declaration of emancipation; and the forbidding of new enslavement. Raffles remains in Malayan history an important precursor.

An ardent emancipator living at Malacca in the 1820's was J. H. Moor, journalist and editor of the Malacca *Observer* from 1826 to 1829 and the Singapore *Chronicle* from 1834 to 1837. For his exposé of the system of slavery which then prevailed in Malacca he "incurred the disapprobation of Government." The agitation, however, had its effect. At a public meeting in 1829 the residents of Malacca committed themselves to freeing all slaves by 1842. In March 1830 a proclamation was issued by the Government in Sangapore saying that the attention of the Governor in Council had lately been called to the practice which prevailed in the Eastern Settlements of importing persons under the denomination of slave-debtors but which in reality was only a cover to actual slave-dealing. Such transactions were henceforth declared to be illegal in a British Colony. The carriers of the trade . . . were Bugis traders, the importers were Chinese in Singapore and the purchasers Chinese in Malacca.

While emancipation was ardently pursued the system of slavery from which the slaves were to be emancipated was not one of unmitigated evil. Raffles has drawn the line that divides the system of "regulated domestic servitude" from the "detestable system which [was] suppressed in the West Indies." There is too the realization of human need involved, the need for women "who supplied the deficiency in the females population and probably in the main became the concubines, if not indeed the wives of leading Chinese and others."

In 1842 Governor [S. G.] Bonham issued his notification "that the last remnant of slavery which existed in the British Settlements in the Straits of Malacca has been for ever abolished by the unanimous accord of the inhabitants themselves." This was a sequel to the public meeting of 1829 which had committed slave-owning residents of Malacca to complete emancipation by 1842, and was "to remove from the minds of the few slaves who may yet be in existence, all apprehension or doubt of their right henceforth to be considered as free and no longer slaves under any denomination colour or pretence whatever."

Some indication of the prevalence of slavery and the slave trade in early Penang may be gleaned from [Captain Francis] Light's first reports. One particularly obnoxious type was the purchase of female slaves for prostitution or "for their own use" by the Bengali sepoys. The trade returns for 1792 valued the import of forty-six slaves at $1,840. The Company itself owned 3,292 "coffrees" (negro slaves or seamen).

An early use of slaves in Penang was to open lands for the cultivation of pepper. The occasional humane observation was that such tasks "should be carried on by free people." But there was no question of its legality as property, hence the injunction that "slaves belonging to ships occasionally reporting to the island gaining their freedom, be delivered up on sufficient proof of their being the property of the claimants."

As Benson Maxwell complained in 1859, the Government of Penang did more than tacitly allow slavery. It provided registers for its transactions in the same legal category as real estate. It also owned slaves. The report for the year 1801-2 gives the number of slaves on the island to be above 1,200 persons. By 1805 the number had increased to 1,400 and a proposal was made that a duty might be imposed on their import. There is no indication that the proposal was approved or implemented, nor was it possible to do so after Lord Grenville's Act came into force in 1807.

This indirectly imposed an obligation on the Presidency Government to liberate all its own slaves as well as to provide for the gradual emancipation of those belonging to the residents of Penang.

## The Malay States

During the first phase of the post-intervention period in the State of Perak the British were much pre-occupied with the failings of Abdullah, which [Governor Sir William F. D.] Jervois described in a long despatch reporting and justifying his appointment of Queen's Commissioners [to advise the sultans]:

(a) collecting slave women, prostitutes and concubines
(b) smoking opium
(c) levying illegal taxes
(d) duplicity in his dealings with the British Government
(e) surrounding himself with bad advisers
(f) borrowing money from the Chinese and spending it in an extravagant manner
(g) hindering the Resident's endeavours to improve the condition of Perak. . . .

There is little recorded evidence of the rôle, if any, that native chiefs played in the work of emancipation, except the brief notes which appear as minutes of the Perak Council Meetings. In the initial period they must have shown some opposition. One incident is recorded. When Raja Yusof, the Regent, attempted to resist [adviser Hugh] Low's order in 1878 for the compulsory registration of all slaves, Low . . . stood no nonsense. "I advised him strongly on the contrary . . . he grudgingly and unwillingly consented to be guided by my opinion which he asked for and obtained in writing."

As Low continued his policy of cajolery, conciliation and generous gifts to needy chiefs, native resistance, if it had existed before, was worn or bribed away.

And though Raja Dris, Dato' Raja Mahkota and the Temenggong in the State Council argued for the period of grace to be extended to 1884 before final emancipation was declared in

Perak, no rejection of emancipation was recorded. In the event the date 31 December 1883 proposed by . . . Low in 1882 remained unchanged. After final acceptance by the chiefs, other resolutions soon followed providing for the compensation of slave-owners. A manumission rate was fixed at the maximum sum of $30 for a male slave or debtor slave and $60 for a female. Between the time of resolution in council, 9 October 1882, and emancipation day, 31 December, 1883 slaves who remained in the service of their owners or creditors would have their services valued at half the sum necessary for manumission. All outstanding sums due on the day of emancipation would be paid by the Government, i.e. at the maximum rate of $15 for a male and $30 for a female.

Thus was effected Hugh Low's maxim that "it would be unjust to deprive the Perak Malays of a property to which by immemorial custom they have been entitled without fair compensation."

In Pahang, as in Perak and Penang, slaves were registered and transferred, not unlike titles to land, during transition period, and their ownership was recognized as an integral part of Malay custom. The measures adopted had in view the eventual abolition of slavery, and provided another example of arbitrary interpretation of the rather vague agreements and exchanges of letters through which the residential system of British administration in the Malay States was established. The 1888 exchange of letters with the Bendahara of Pahang, which specifically provided for the non-interference in Malay custom, brought about . . . regulations on slavery to end "a national custom" of the Malays. The chief point about the legislation against slavery was not its legality but nineteenth-century English morality, and it was never fully implemented.

However, . . . it was fully in accord with the Islamic laws of human behaviour. Further, the Resident was careful to act through the Sultan and in his name, thus acting in accordance with the law of the state though not entirely with the letter of the agreement with the Sultan. . . .

Captain Bloomfield Douglas, a much underrated British Resident, had a rather different approach to slavery in Selangor. In the view of the Sultan, the Selangor laws did not acknowledge slavery in any shape, Douglas reported in 1878. And though it had become a custom of the land, slaves, where they were found in Selangor, were not normally ill-treated. "Thus," argued Douglas "all slavery should be quietly dropped and ignored." There was no need for public notice or proclamation, nor was it worth a discussion in the State Council. It was "more expedient to let it die out quietly than to make it appear the Residential system was in any way to change the old institutions of the country." Consequently no legislation was passed on slavery in Selangor and the minutes of the State Council contain no reference to it. The Resident confined himself to issuing instructions empowering the magistrates to free all slave-debtors after a due assessment of the value of labour already given to the creditor.

The principle adopted was "to set the total term of work done against the original debt proved" either as the purchase price for a slave or as the loan of a slave-debtor. This had the effect of virtually freeing the slaves when they came before the magistrates.

If Weld, writing in 1882, was accurate in his observation, the problem was less to free the slaves from their debts than to free them from themselves. They were reluctant to leave the security assured to them by their masters or creditors for the doubtful privilege of being free "which involved greater exertion."

In this connexion Martin Lister's remarks in his Report for 1887 on Negri Sembilan are pertinent:

> In the inland States of the Sri Menanti a man's wealth is calculated by his paddy fields and buffaloes. Cessation from the cultivation of his fields is a source of shame not only to him, but to his wife. It is by this means that it is feasible in Sri Menanti, unlike the other Native States, to abolish debt slavery, ameliorate the condition of former slaves in comparison with emancipation in which case they would be penniless, and at the same time preserve them to their original masters for the cultivation of their lands. There is little or no cruelty to slave debtors in Sri Menanti, and the cases are few and

> far betwen where the former slaves apply for unconditional emancipation which, except in very special cases, should not be granted in the interest of the slave debtors themselves.

A more recent observation from one whose boyhood was spent in a home that owned slaves in East Pahang explains further the reluctance of slaves to leave their master.

> . . . the slaves did not find it convenient to leave their master's land. They had no land of their own. They were so used to depending upon rations . . . supplied by their master. Remunerative employment was not available anywhere. Some of the older ones had become really attached to their masters, enjoying most of the benefits, but avoiding much of the work.[1]

In Kedah debt-bondage "sanctioned by Immemorial custom" remained an important system of labour employment in 1910. The English attitude represented by men like George Maxwell, who arived in Kedah as its first British Advisor, was against its continuance since debtor-labour tended to be "indolent and improvident . . . expensive, dangerous and demoralising." Earlier Captain James Low in 1836 described it as a system which fostered idleness and suppressed ambition. Maxwell worked for its abolition. In 1910 the State Council favoured abolishing the system, but unanimously agreed that abolition was not then a practical proposition. Instead, "the State Council approved a system under which all these debts would be invalid unless they were registered, and all debts would be automatically reduced every month by a fixed sum in lieu of salary." With this object the Debt-bondage Enactment dated 18 July 1910 was passed. All debts not registered would be declared illegal after 1 December 1910. Further, creditors after that date would have no claim on the labour of future debtors. In effect the system was abolished, though the existing registered claims of creditors on the labour of their debtors were recognized. . . .

For the calculation of registered debts a menial servant's labour was valued at $2.50 per month, a padi planter at $2 for every relong of land planted, and an orchard caretaker at $2 a month.

The sequel to this is best recorded by Maxwell himself:

> Within a couple of years of the enactment coming into force, some debtors won their freedom and either left their employers, or as often happened, stayed on with them as free salaried servants. This was hardly noticed by the general public; and then every month, in increasing numbers, more and more debtors won their freedom. By this time every one realised that the system was nearing its end and the State Treasury had been keeping a careful record of every debt and of the amount still due by the debtors. One day, when the State Council was dealing with the Public Works Department's estimates, and was approving considerable sums . . . I asked Tunku Mahmud whether he had any idea of the total amount due by all the debt-bondsmen and women in the State. When I gave the figure supplied by the State Treasury, every one was amazed by its being not more than some of the items which we had been cheerfully passing for the P.W.D. I then said, "Shall we pass a vote now and pay off all the creditors and put an end to this thing?" This was unanimously approved with acclamation. Proclamations were issued the next day that all these debtors were free, and that the creditors would be paid the amount due to them upon application to the Treasury.[2]

"In legislation," wrote Disraeli in 1874, "it is not merely reason and propriety which are to be considered, but the temper of the time." In retrospect, the legislation on slavery in Malaya reflects this dictum. . . .

It is apparent that much of the success of the British approach to slavery rests in the persistent effort of men like Hugh Low to observe the original contract which protected not only persons but also property. The recognition of slaves as property, at least for the period of transition, may be attributed to the exigencies of the time. It was time then for the British to reassure the Malay ruling class that their preesnce did not mean a confiscation of customary status. But there is a wider outlook which regarded the rights of property as sacred. John Locke in a much earlier time laid down his priority of rights wherein property takes precedence over the right of life itself. . . .

Property therefore became the bedrock of emancipation in the Malay States, and Freedom was carefully bought. One of the benefits of the introduction of a money economy based on tin was to provide the cash to free the debtors and slaves. Its more important significance, however, lies in its provision of work for the freed and in that way freed them, not only from their indebtedness, but also from almost total dependence on their masters.

## NOTES

1. Dato Mahmud bin Mat, "The Passing of Slavery in East Pahang," *The Malayan Historical Journal*, (May, 1954), p. 10.
2. Sir George Maxwell, "Memories of the First British Advisor, Kedah," *Malaya in History*, IV (July, 1958), p. 14.

# 4

# THE SLAVE TRADE TODAY

Slavery continues today. The United Nations has ordered investigations of slavery in the Near East, and reports from Saudi Arabia, Pakistan, and elsewhere of the sale of slaves, usually children, are not uncommon. While now tiny, the Anti-Slavery and Aborigines' Protection Society continues to function from its quarters in Denison House on Vauxhall Bridge Road in London, and voices—most often British—still ask, What are we going to do about this matter? One such voice has been Baron Shackleton (1911-      ), O.B.E., son of the famous explorer, leader of the House of Lords since 1968. In July, 1960, he addressed the House on the question of slavery in Africa and Arabia. In the 1970's he has continued to remind the world of the realities of slavery as practiced near the Indian Ocean littoral.

Lord Shackleton rose to ask her Majesty's Government what information they have on the continued existence of slavery, particularly in Africa and Arabia; what steps they propose to take to ensure the implementation of international conventions designed to bring this inhuman and degrading practice to an end, if necessary by the establishment of a special organization within the United Nations, and whether they will raise this urgent problem at the July meeting of the Economic and Social Council of the United Nations. The noble Lord said: My Lords, we have just been discussing one of the new scourges of humanity, and I rise to ask the Question standing in my name in order to draw attention to one of the most ancient scourges that have afflicted mankind. It was only last year that the bicentenary of the birth of William Wilberforce was commemorated, and your Lordships are well aware that his Parliamentary life was mainly devoted to the abolition of slavery and that his work has been carried on by many able people since. It is now the general impression among people in this country that slavery no longer exists, and the object of my Question is not only to draw attention to the amount of slavery that there is in the world but to ask the Government what information they have from their sources upon this subject, and, in particular, to ask what steps they propose to take by way of international action or by other means to put an end to this degrading business.

There is no need, I think, to go into the history of slavery. I think it is universally accepted that, however well a slave may be treated, none the less it is in every way a repugnant basis of life for mankind. And of course European nations have no reason to be mealy-mouthed on this subject, or to be proud of the part they have played. We know that some of the great civilisations in classical times were built on slavery and that many European nations have played their part in the slave trade. But we do not need to waste time on the past. Our problem is to consider what there is in the way of slavery in the world today and what ought to be done to end it.

. . . The chief centre of slavery in the world is still the Arabian Peninsula, and in particular Saudi Arabia, where it is estimated—and I must stress that it is only an estimate, and may be a very rough one—that there may be as many as half a million slaves today. My remarks will be mainly concerned with the slave trade as it relates to the Arabian Peninsula. It is the one region where the old chattel slavery still exists and is recognised as a legal status.

The countries of Arabia have theocratic government, and in them the law of the land is the *Koran*, which is supplemented by decrees made by the rulers. Slave owners and defenders of slavery—and this is important, because people are inclined to think that we should allow people to pursue their own historic customs—have argued that slavery is authorised by the *Koran* and by the teachings of the Prophet Mohammed, but the weight of evidence, I am told, is against this. Mohammed tolerated slavery in the backward community in which he lived, but at the same time he condemned it and intended that it should be progressively suppressed. Islamic writers of authority have stated in on uncertain terms that if the teachings of Mohammed on slavery had been applied in all Moslem countries, slavery would have ceased to exist, not only, as it has, in some of them, but in all. It is still practised not merely in Arabia but also the Yemen, Muscat, Oman and the small sheikhdoms and sultanates in the Aden Protectorate. There is an abundance of evidence from unofficial sources from travellers and residents in Saudi Arabia and those countries, that slavery exists there, and may, indeed, be increasing.

In 1936 the late King Ibn Saud of Saudi Arabia made a decree regulating the conditions of slaves. This decree largely restated the teachings of the *Koran*, requiring masters to be kind to their slaves. It also gave slaves certain rights to buy their freedom and, above all, it required slave owners to register their slaves with the Government. But while the principal aim was to help slaves throughout their servitude, as well as to provide some prospect of freedom, it also authorised, as I have said, the licensing of slave traders. That decree is still law, and there is plenty of evidence that the law is fully taken advantage of. This decree makes clear that it is part of the accepted pattern of life in those countries.

I should like to quote some of the further evidence that exists. Some of it is, I admit, old evidence, although collected in the last few years, and some of it may be already familiar to your Lordships. One of our difficulties, of course, is to get official, up-to-date information. There is evidence supplied not only by ministers. There was one which, I know, has already been quoted in this House. A French Protestant minister actually went to investigate rumours of slavery in French Africa and he reported in 1955 what he had found. In his report there is a dispatch written by the French Ambassador in Saudi Arabia. He stated that slave traders in Saudi Arabia were sending African emissaries to Africa to recruit slaves. They went and posed as Moslem missionaries and offered Africans a free pilgrimage to Mecca, which they said was being paid for by rich Moslems who had sinned and sought atonement in this way. Many Africans in the past few years have fallen into this trap. On arrival in Saudi Arabia they have been arrested for entering without a visa, and have been imprisoned and handed over to slave traders. The French Ambassador estimated the number who suffered that fate at a few hundred a year. The Government of Nigeria has since taken steps to try to limit this by licensing travel agencies, particularly those who deal with the Arabian countries.

There is, indeed, plenty of evidence, also coming from the same source, of African Moslems going on pilgrimages and taking several servants with them whom they sell on arrival, using them as living traveller's cheques. It is astonishing that faithful Moslems who believe in the teachings of their Prophet, can sit back and allow, if not connive at, the holy places of Islam being used to lure innocent Africans into slavery. There are numerous examples, too, some of them from official sources, of the actual practice of slavery in particular areas. . . .

If anybody were to suggest that these slaves were always well treated, I would draw attention to a case, again well-founded, of twelve Baluchi slaves, some of whom were the personal property of the King of Saudi Arabia, who tried to escape. They were discovered, tracked down, and three were beheaded in the desert by the search party; others were brought back to Riyadh for public execution, where they were duly beheaded by a negro slave whose name was Al Hilali, in the square in front of the palace, to provide a lesson to other would-be escapees. . . .

There are other areas in the world where slavery is practised. A Danish ethnologist has described the practice of slavery among the Tuaregs of the Sahara, and my noble friend Lord Maugham, who is shortly to speak, has some much more up-to-date and direct personal experience of this area. There is evidence collected by the Anti-Slavery [and Aborigines' Protection] Society through Commander [G. H.] Fox-Pitt, who went to West Africa and himself found plenty of evidence of this practice.

Finally, there has been some quite horrifying evidence of slavery in South America, in particular in Peru. . . . There has been slavery in China, although there is information that the new Chinese Government is taking strong steps to wipe it out. . . .

I should like now to turn to the legal and international position with regard to slavery. The first really effective international action was taken in the Brussels Slavery Convention in 1890. This was effective because it had machinery written into it for supervising its application. It is possible that this Convention may still be in force, but it would probably be difficult to resuscitate because some of the signatories, like the Austro-Hungarian Empire, no longer exist. After the First World War the Slavery Convention of 1926 was signed under the auspices of the League of Nations. This contained no machinery for supervision. It was not until after the efforts, largely of British initiative, of men like the noble Viscount, Lord Cecil of Chelwood, Charles Roden Buxton and others, that a special Committee was set up, which was successful to a considerable degree in not only collecting evidence but gradually reducing the slave traffic.

I emphasize the phrase "slave traffic." It is a question not only of the existence of slavery in countries where there are already slaves, but of a continuing traffic, going on from different parts of Africa. After the last war a new Convention was set up on the advice of a committee of experts. This was signed in 1956. It lacks any machinery for supervising its application. . . .

My Lords, I should like to ask what Her Majesty's Government are going to do about this matter. . . .

# 5

# INVOLUNTARY LABOR SINCE ABOLITION

If there is no guaranteed source of labor, will men find other means of filling such a need? Was slavery merely a phase in a constant search for manpower that would be stable, readily available, and cheap? As slavery was abolished, did industrial society find means of replacing the peculiar institution with other forms of involuntary servitude that still kept a larger portion of mankind among Frantz Fanon's "wretched of the earth?" What conditions give rise to the need for mass labor and what conditions lead societies to condone inforced means of finding a supply? We do not have all of the answers to these questions, but we have some suggestions. These are brought together in the concluding selection that follows, taken from a thesis submitted to the University of Amsterdam by Willemina Kloosterboer (1925- ), a Dutch scholar now affiliated with the State University of Utrecht. Published in English translation in Holland in 1960, this work drew upon the insights of an earlier Dutch scholar, H. J. Nieboer. His arguments, summarized below, show an interesting parallel to the thesis put forward in 1893 by the American historian, Frederick Jackson Turner, on the significance of the frontier in American history, by which Turner explained the genesis of American democratic institutions. One might end with the question, therefore, did the very forces which helped to provide America with its democratic ethos work to exclude the black man from that ethos? For an insightful exploration of some of the implications of Nieboer's argument, the reader should also consult Eugene Genovese, *The Political Economy of Slavery* (New York, 1967).

The Dutch author H. J. Nieboer, in his thesis *Slavery as an Industrial System* (1900),* indicated that the occurrence or non-occurrence of slavery in a society is dependent on the economic state of that society. Slavery as a rule will not exist if the circumstances—which he seeks particularly in the land situation—are such that there is an offer of voluntary labour. On the other hand, if this voluntary labour is not available, then, in most instances, slavery will occur.

The abolition of negro slavery in the course of the 19th century would appear in the light of this theory to have been premature. Generally speaking, the circumstances in the colonies at the time were not such that an offer of sufficient voluntary labour could be anticipated. But then it was in fact so that the impetus for abolition came from groups not directly involved in slavery. The slave-holders themselves were violently opposed to abolition, and, being overruled, it was not long before they substituted new forms of compulsory labour.

It is indeed not clear why precisely slavery should exist if there is not sufficient voluntary labour. As labour systems, serfage, debt-slavery, and even contract labour under penal sanction fulfil exactly the same function. The form compulsory labour takes will in the first place depend on the spirit of the times. Public opinion in the West would never have approved of the re-institution of slavery as such after abolition, no matter how acute the labour shortage. In these circumstances, however, other forms of compulsory labour were resorted to—often leaving the victims not much better off than before.

---

* Revised edition, The Hague, 1910.

. . . In a certain sense almost all labour can be classed as compulsory; by far the majority of people do after all work out of necessity to support themselves and not because they are particularly keen to. But this is not the sort of compulsion we are concerned with here. In our society everyone may at least decide for himself whether he would rather work for his bread or not work and starve. No direct external compulsion is exerted. . . .

. . . [W]e will examine the phenomenon of compulsory labour (since the abolition of slavery) in the light of Nieboer's theory, as presented in his "Slavery as an Industrial System." The main argument of his theory can be expressed as follows: Slavery will generally occur where there is still free land available (through which a livelihood can be found without the help of capital), where there are, in other words, still "open resources." In areas where there is no longer any free land available (or where capital, not available to all, is necessary to provide subsistence), thus where there are "closed resources," there will on the contrary generally be no slavery, since in the latter case there will generally be people prepared to work for wages (not being able to support themselves independently) and slavery thus becomes superfluous. Where there are "open resources," however, no one is dependent on another for his earnings, and it is therefore necessary to use force if others are to be made to work for an individual. The author discusses slavery in his book, but not other forms of compulsory labour, although he does occasionally refer to these as disguised slavery to which his theory is also applicable. Indeed one cannot see why, under the circumstances mentioned by Nieboer, it should be precisely slavery that exists if there is not a sufficient offer of voluntary labour, and not another form of compulsory labour. . . . If Nieboer's thesis is valid, then the realities of compulsory labour other than slavery will be in agreement with it. . . .

In the West Indies—with the exception of Antigua—complete freedom was not immediately granted to all slaves in 1834. Only children under the age of six were freed. For the remaining Negroes an apprenticeship system was introduced, which in effect meant that the former slaves were now compelled to work for their former holders without payment for a further number of years; in most cases six years but in a few instances four. The holders, however, no longer had complete rights over their former slaves. A few directives were given. For example, a maximum number of working hours was determined; 45 hours a week for "apprentices" in agriculture—and these were in the majority. It was hoped that they would offer to work for wages in their spare time; and to encourage this it was decreed that "apprentices" could buy their freedom from further services at a fixed price.

Under this system the former slaves could not as yet consider themselves particularly well off. As is to be expected the planters were not always of good will, and the Government in London had to be continually taking action to bring about improvements in the colonial legislation, especially against the legislative body in Jamaica, where almost half the Negroes on the British West Indies lived. Cruelties frequently occurred both on the plantations and in the prisons where they amounted to atrocities; so much so that various members of the Anti[-]Slavery Society—disbanned after abolition became a reality—felt obliged to take up action again.

However, the apprenticeship system was only intended as a first step to complete freedom, and we will leave it at that. In fact it came to an end in 1838, which was for most "apprentices" two years earlier than at first intended, whilst on one of the islands, Antigua, the planters had preferred to declare complete freedom for all the Negroes right from scratch in 1834.

A dire shortage of plantation labourers arose as soon as the apprenticeship system came to an end. The Negroes did not feel much inclined to work, and especially not on the plantations since to their minds slave-driving was an inherent factor in such labour. In the beginning all wished to be free and the result was chaos. Although this state of affairs sorted itself out to some extent later it still remained extremely difficult for the planters to find labourers. Where there was little density of population and much uncultivated land, as in British Guiana, Jamaica and Trinidad, the more energetic Negroes were in a position to buy their own plots of ground with the money they had been able to save in their time as "apprentices." Many, desiring a change, decided on other forms of labour, becoming shopkeepers, small merchants, fishermen and even carriers; and frequently those parents who stayed on at the plantations would send their children to the towns. And all this mainly, because of the association between plantation labour and slavery. Even from those who stayed on at the plantations, or returned there after some time, not much work was to be expected since they could, with the produce of the small holdings which had been theirs of old, either support their families entirely or manage, if the plots were too small, by adding the wages of a few days' labour a week. . . .

Under these difficult circumstances the planters attempted in various ways to get a better hold on their labourers. The settlers in Antigua were first faced with this problem, having, as already stated, not felt much for the introduction of an apprenticeship system in 1834. Within a few months of abolition a law called the Contract Act was passed on this island and enforced in anticipation of approval from London. By this act Negro labour was drastically regulated.

As soon as a contract was concluded between planter and labourer the following stipulations applied:

1. If the labourer was absent from work for half a day or less (!) without good cause he forfeited his wage for the whole day.
2. If he was absent for two consecutive days, or for two days in fourteen, he was liable to a week's imprisonment with hard labour.
3. For negligence of various kinds during work he could be convicted to up to three months hard labour.

The employer on the other hand was only liable for breach of contract to a maximum fine of £5. What is more, even a verbal contract made in the presence of two witnesses was considered valid.

Although it is true that the Government of the mother country did not accept the regulation in this form, it did pass it with a few modifications; and in its final form the act contained a remarkable clause stating that the occupation of a tenement entailed on a Negro the same obligations as the conclusion of a verbal labour contract. It is clear that this, on an island where there was as good as no uncultivated land left, amounted to forced labour for the greater part of the Negro population.

For many years this law was in force in Antigua, and through it the labour situation there became much more favourable for the planters than on the other islands. For when the labour problem arose elsewhere a few years later the home country was no longer prepared to sanction similar measures.

Even without the Contract Act, however, ways and means were found of imposing plantation labour on part of the Negroes. Many of the Negro families, who for generations had had the use of shacks and small holdings on the plantations, were now made to pay for the privilege of this occupation in labour and not in money, as would have been reasonable in a system of voluntary labour. As a rule only the head of the family was obliged to work, but then he had to do so almost continuously. On Barbados, for example, it was customary to demand nine hours a day five days a week. In some instances all members of the family had to assist. On the densely populated islands the planters speculated with this measure realizing how little opportunity the Negro had of moving away, but mainly—and this applied everywhere—banking on the Negro's attachment to his shack and small holding.

More than half the Negroes of the British West Indies lived in Jamaica, and here it was that abolition was most stubbornly opposed by the planters. After its realization they were not content to make the Negro work for his use of a small holding, but so regulated the matter that the wage worked out at less than the rent of the tenement. In this way the people were more or less faced with a form of debt slavery.

Moreover, in 1840 a law was passed in Jamaica against "vagrancy. A "vagrant" according to this law was any man who migrated from his home leaving his wife and children unprovided for. In the absence of a police officer, it was decreed that anyone could arrest such a person. Thus another attempt at hindering the migration of Negroes from the plantations.

In Mauritius, however, the settlers went much further in their endeavours to keep the Negroes at work after abolition became a reality on February 1st, 1835, six months later than in the West

Indies. Even in the same year an ordinance was passed whereby the greater majority of the population were faced with a situation hardly to be considered as any better than slavery. The main clauses of the ordinance read as follows:

All persons under the age of sixty years, capable of labour [that is, women as well as men] and unable to prove that they follow a business or possess suffiicent means of subsistence, shall be bound to take up a trade, or find employment, or hire themelves as field labourers, within a period to be fixed by the police. In the event of failure to perform this duty, the offender is to be delivered to the police to be employed on the public works. And if after three months any such person shall not have found employment, he may be sentenced to be placed on a plantation or in a factory, to be three employed for a period not exceeding three years. . . . And one's troubles were not necessarily over after three years of forced labour since a following clause decreed that anyone who had not found other work after completion of this term could again be put to work in the same way. It was made difficult, if not impossible, for the labourer to find new work by a further clause holding anyone guilty of enticing a labourer away from the plantation of his holder liable to pay damages and a fine. A comprehensive registration of all labourers, coupled with a decree making it compulsory for every labourer to carry on his person an identification card issued by the police (and to be renewed with every change of employer), made it even more difficult for them, particularly seeing that these regulations were most rigorously and unsympathetically enforced. In fact someone even temporarily unemployed could find himself convicted to forced labour despite his not having committed any crime, and his chances of ever getting away from the plantation to which the police sent him were very slender indeed.

One can imagine that this state of affairs did not improve the way in which the planter (till shortly before, slave-holder) treated his labourers. Furthermore, a labourer who attacked his master or his master's representative was, in terms of the ordinance, liable to a maximum of 12 months' imprisonment, with or without hard labour. And if three or more labourers should collaborate in an attempt to leave the plantation or improve the conditions of labour, they would be liable to six months hard labour. In addition one later had to work two days longer for every day spent in jail.

Finally it was even made possible in the ordinance to put children over eight to work as apprentices up to their 21st year. And, because it could apparently not be taken for granted that the ordinance as it stood would be sufficient to bring the free population to work, another clause was introduced by which contraventions of any kind by unemployed persons could be all the more heavily penalized. A farther going system of labour compulsion is hardly imaginable.

When the ordinance was sent to the Minister of Colonial Affairs for approval he was singularly dismayed, and, to the indignation of the Governor, the Council and planters of Mauritius, he promptly turned it down. In the meantime the ordinance had already been in force for almost a year and . . . many of the clauses found their way into the legislation in the course of the following years, although they then mainly pertained to another section of the population. . . .

In those territories where the labour shortage remained acute the planters were quick to seek a solution in another direction entirely. Both in the West Indies and Mauritius they started drawing labour from elsewhere. The first attempt in the West Indies, with Portuguese from Madeira and Negroes from the West Coast of Africa, proved unsuccessful. Results were satisfactory only when the planters started importing Indians, and—in the West Indies—small numbers of Chinese. Indeed in the end the labour problem was in fact solved in this way.

Indians started arriving in large numbers in Mauritius soon after abolition. In the West Indies a stop was put to the immigration after an initial start in 1838, but by 1844 a regular stream of Indian coolies started arriving here too. Chinese emigration was mainly to British Guiana, and the greater proportion arrived between 1853 and 1874. In all about 450,000 Indians emigrated to Mauritius, 200,000 to British Guiana and 150,000 to Trinidad (far fewer to the other West Indian islands). About 16,000 Chinese arrived in British Guiana. The immigration of British Indians continued for many years. On Mauritius it ended in 1911, when there were a sufficient number of labourers on the island. In 1917, at the proposal of the Government of India, the British Government prohibited all immigration of contract labourers.

This Indian and Chinese immigration followed the pattern of the indentured-labour system by which the emigrants signed a contract in India or China committing themselves to work, usually for a full 5 year period, in the country to which they were sent. They received free passage and the contractors were required to provide regular work at reasonable wages as well as housing and medical attention. In the West Indies the immigrants also had the right on a free passage, or (later) partly free passage, back to the country of origin after working a number of years, mostly ten.

Most characteristic of this Indian and Chinese labour, however, was the penal sanction: Contrary to what we know in Western law, there were criminal laws to cover breach of contract. Desertion and absence from work, and even negligence of various kinds, was punishable, often with imprisonment. This gave to this labour an involuntary aspect. After all there was no way of terminating one's service when one wished, no matter how unhappy the circumstances. And the involuntary nature of this contract labour was considerably enhanced by the way in which the labourers were recruited and put to work, and the way in which the coolies were sometimes kept on even after the contract period had expired. . . .

. . . [I]n British Guiana . . . there existed for him the possibility of being shipped back to his own country after a period of ten years, i.e. five years after completion of his first contract period. If, however, he were to remain in British Guiana he would find very little opportunity to support himself other than as a plantation labourer. There was no regulation making it possible for him to acquire land of his own, and, although trading and handcrafts were open to all, the opportunities here were very limited. It was possible however to become a free plantation labourer.

In fact by about 1870 there were from 8,000 to 9,000 free Indians in British Guiana as opposed to from 17,000 to 18,000 who had signed up for a second period of five years on completion of their first term of service. But only the cleverest, who had succeeded in saving some money, were able to become free. The majority had no option but to sign up again for a further period.

The colonists devised ways and means of exercising pressure to achieve this end, in the first place by granting a not unreasonable sum of money on renewal of a contract, but also by violent insistence. This insistence came not only from the planters but from the immigration agents as well. . . .

However, the coolie's position in Mauritius was even more unfavourable. Here too pressure was applied on the coolies to make them sign again, and here too much use was made of the law as an instrument of pressure. As in Guiana, a coolie would be promised freedom of legal consequences if he signed up for a further period. That was one method, another was to bring the coolie who refused to sign before the magistrate for every petty offence in the hope that he would in this way eventually yield. But the worst of all was that even those who had freed themselves of contract labour despite all this pressure were not yet left in peace. As early as 1844 a regulation was passed defining a "vagrant" as someone able but unwilling to work, becoming thereby a menace to society and because of it liable to a maximum of 28 days imprisonment; which term was later extended to 6 to 9 months on repetition. In 1867, however, a new and much more stringent regulation came into force which in reality entailed compulsory labour for all Indians.

Every old immigrant no longer working under contract had in future to be in possession of a valid pass only issued by the police if it could be shown by the applicant that he was in regular employ. An immigrant whose contract had expired and who did not wish to sign up again had to be in possession of such a pass within 8 days (in special circumstances 15 days), which is to say that he had in that time to ensure himself of new employment. If this period was transgressed he was liable to a fine of £2 or 7 days imprisonment. Somebody found without a pass was taken to the immigration depot where he had to prove that he was executing work of one sort or another. Should he not succeed in satisfying the authorities on this point he would be looked upon as a "vagrant" and treated as such. The police had the power with the approval of the authorities concerned to enter immigrants' dwellings to examine all passes. On top of all this it was decreed that immigrants were not allowed to move out of their districts, except in special circumstances, the reason being that such a measure would simplify control. Somebody found outside his own district could be arrested and brought to the immigration depot wheer his case would be examined. All in all, a remarkably stringent regulation!

And it was applied as severely as possible. In fact the immigrants were hunted down in the same way as had been customary in the days of slavery. An Indian walking in the streets stood a great chance of being held up by a policeman, and—as was often the case—if the policeman could not read the pass, which was written out in English, he would simply take him along to the police station. The magistrates cooperated with the police in applying the law as strictly as possible, and it was not a rare occurrence for an immigrant to be convicted as a vagrant even though actively employed. In addition, it should be borne in mind that after 1852 the immigrants had no rights whatever on a free or even partly free passage back to their own country. They were thus entirely at the mercy of the colonists and the lives they led during and after the contract period did not differ all that much from slavery. . . .

In another British colony of the time, the Cape Colony, abolition of the slave-trade in 1807 might almost be said to have produced greater turmoil than slave emancipation did in 1834. For here the natives of the territory, primarily Hottentots, were not used as slaves, whereas there had been a regular traffic of slaves for some 150 years from Madagascar and Mozambique, and from British and Netherlands India. Cutting off this source of supply left the farmers with labour problems, and it was at this point that they looked to the natives as a possible labour force.

These . . . were mainly Hottentots. With the advent of the Dutch they were by degrees robbed of their land, and by about 1800 there was no land available for them any longer to lead their former nomadic existence. They either roamed the country aimlessly, feeding off wild vegetation, or lived on the land of the Europeans. Some of this last group were put to work by the Boers, but, since they showed little inclination to work and since there were sufficient slaves about, many among them did little to no work.

By 1807, when the slave-trade came to an end, the colonists felt little obliged to tolerate all this, and in 1809 regulations were passed with a view to altering the situation. Every Hottentot had in future to have a "place of fixed abode." Migration was not permissible without a pass issued by the specified authorities. Anybody found roaming about without this pass would be picked up as a "vagrant" and allocated to a farmer as a labourer; and it was the duty of every European to demand to see the pass of any suspect "vagrant."

By these measures the Hottentots were in reality forced to enter the employ of the Europeans. After all, the "place of fixed abode" could hardly be on land of their own since they no longer had any, and neither was roaming from place to place possible any longer. . . .

. . . [Thus] the abolition of slavery did not necessarily mean the end of compulsory labour, other forms havin been evolved wherever this seemed necessary or advantageous from an economic point of view.

In Spanish America, enslavement of the Indians was forbidden (except in certain specific caes) from the very outset of colonization. Nevertheless, other forms of compulsory labour were instituted. To start with, the Indians were divided among the Spaniards who could then dispose of their labour, for comparatively short periods at first, but longer periods for later generations (the *encomienda* system). When this system became inadequate after some time—newcomers finding that there were no Indians available for them—it was abolished, to be immediately replaced by another form of compulsory labour. Now every Indian village had to deliver a stipulated number of labourers to an entrepreneur—the labourers being chosen in rotation from among the inhabitants. When this system (called *repartimiento* or *mita*) became in its turn no longer economical—the system of a rotating and primitive labour force no longer being satisfactory in view of the increasing demands for skilled labour—it also disappeared from the scene. But there was something to fill the gap, for by that time debt bondage had become prevalent—and this form of labour compulsion remained to stay. . . .

In Java . . . the set up was different. After the abolition of forced labour under the culture system (more or less synonymous with the abolition of slavery elsewhere) the private planters then appearing in greater numbers had no real difficulty in procuring labourers because of the over-population. But here the difficulty lay in the fact that this labour, once procured, could not be depended upon since the Javanese labourer only worked for as long as he desperately needed the earnings, and as soon as he had a little laid aside he left his employment. It was for this reason that labour compulsion was resorted to, although it was not carried to the same lengths as in other countries where the labour problems were more pressing. Penal sanction, and, after the mother country had repealed that, the creation of debt relationships, and the exercising of pressure through the *desa* chiefs or European officials were, among others, the means used to improve the situation.

In some countries, the extreme measures adopted immediately after abolition were dispensed with fairly soon. Such was the case, . . . in the United States where the "vagrancy" laws, if not entirely abrogated, were at least applied much more leniently. But then, neither did the need for severity last long here. The Negroes did not succeed (except in a few cases) in acquiring small farms of their own, and, since there were no other ways open to them of becoming independent, they had no other choice but to work for Europeans. Under such circumstances, matters could be left to run their own course. . . .

In the sparsely populated Portuguese colonies there was also, generally speaking, little need for the Africans to work for the Europeans, and here too, compulsory labour persisted, the early legislative measures remaining in force and being made even harsher from time to time.

However, in many territories a great advance in the economic life, bringing wit it a great need for a labour force, occurred a long time after the abolition of slavery. This was, for example, the case in South Africa (where the really great demand for labour first arose with the exploitation of diamonds and gold after 1870), in the Outer Provinces of the Dutch East Indies (where large-scale colonization began at about the same time), and in Kenya (where the Europeans only began to come in large numbers at the beginning of this century). Similarly, at the turn of the century, there was also a switch to large-scale economic activity in the Congo Free State, and in those regions of Latin America where rubber was obtainable, the rapidly rising demand for this product creating an urgent need for labour in distant, sparsely populated country. And the French were faced with the same difficulty when they took over the administration of Madagascar in 1896 (i.e., almost 50 years after they had abolished slavery), and wished to develop it.

. . . [C]ompulsory labour was resorted to in all these cases, sometimes ruthlessly—if the difficulties were great and there seemed no other solution (e.g., the rubber regions in Latin America, and, to a lesser extent, Kenya and Madagascar)—sometimes more subtly—as for example in the Outer Provinces of the Dutch East Indies, where labourers could be drawn from nearby, overpopulated areas—or sometimes even altogether indirectly, as in South Africa where the country itself is heavily populated.

. . . [C]ompulsory labour is not only found in countries where two races of unequal economic power confront each other, such as in the colonial territories, but . . . it has also been applied in some Western countries to the people of the country itself; our prime example being Soviet Russia. To achieve the tremendous economic expansion here, labour compulsion was resorted to; and then not only in the well populated areas—by means of a ban on non-working, the forcible removal of labour forces, etc.—but also in the more inaccessible areas of the North and East which were to be colonized. But Soviet Russia is not the only example, since compulsory labour has also been imposed on whites in the United States, although only in sporadic cases. Here it concerned the development of industries in areas far removed from a source of labour supply (e.g., the Maine lumber companies).

An important factor in these differences in the use of compulsory labour in the United States and Soviet Russia is undeniably the difference of approach to social-economic questions. In a system in which the economy is planned by the state, a severe regulation of labour such as is found in Russia is normal. A general lack of respect for the individual which may occur in such a system can, in special circumstances—when normal methods of providing labour are inadequate for work in distant places with forbidding climate—lead to the worst sort of forced labour. Where *laisser faire* is the social ideal, as in the United States, such a situation (for its own people) is only possible in cases of national emergency, such as war. However, it should not be forgotten that there are other factors besides the social-economic ideals which influence the issue of compulsory labour. In the United States there was a great tide of immigration during the period of industrialization, which to a great extent filled the demand for labour, whereas Russia, when later on industrialization began there, had to draw on its own population resources. Moreover, when we compare the situation in Soviet Russia with that in the Western European countries in their period of developing industry, it is clear that where these countries colonized they needed to provide relatively few people—the native population (not, as a rule, willingly!) supplying the labour requirements—while Soviet Russia used, at a time when she was in the throes of an industrial revolution, its own people (plus those from neighbouring countries) to open up the vast, uninhabited expanses of Asia and Northern Russia. And it is this simultaneous industrialization at a previously unheard of rate on the one hand,. and colonization of vast, uninhabited territories without much help by the native population on the other, which makes the Soviet-Russian situation unique.

As yet we have only spoken of cases where compulsory labour was imposed by whites. However, the whites have not been the only people to resort to the use of this form of labour. In Liberia, for instance, which was founded as a settlement for emancipated slaves from America, these emancipated slaves used the natives of the country in exactly the same way as the Europeans set about using the native populations of their colonies; and in the Negro State of Haiti the rulers, when their subjects showed signs of reverting to a life of idleness, even instituted an official system of forced labour, whereby non-working was not permitted, and strict supervision made hard work unavoidable.

We also learn something else from the history of Haiti. When later Governors dispensed with the use of force the country deteriorated. Under certain circumstances therefore compulsion would appear to be indispensable, at any rate, if the object is to develop a country. In Haiti, it soon became clear that there were no native leaders able to make people work, whereas the whites have never hesitated to make the native populations labour for them wherever they colonized, and their appearance in a new country has led to the introduction of compulsory labour whenever it was profitable—compulsory labour for the authorities *and* for private individuals.

In general, there is less to be said against the former than against the latter. In many cases, its institution can be compared to taation in our society. And if it is not too heavily imposed, and is used for purposes which also serve the interests of the native population it is in most cases carried out without resentment.

However, so much misuse is often made of this system of labour that it can frequently become an almost unbearable burden for the labourers who are in most cases put to work on projects which can make no direct contribution to the welfare of their community; the construction of great highways and railways, for example. Moreover, in most cases, the labourers have to work far too long on these projects, sometimes far from their homes (which factor can only serve to disrupt their lives). . . .

The worst conditions of compulsory labour are of course those where it is nothing but terror which keeps the people at work. The labour of the rubber tappers in South America and the Congo Free State are examples of this; and there was also a strong element of terror in the employment of Angolese Negroes on the islands off the West Coast of Africa.

In conclusion, the question of land shortage. In Java, there was such a large native population that many were unable to acquire land and thereby became available to the Europeans as labourers. More often, the natives would have to go to work because of a land shortage after the whites had taken over all the good land for themselves, . . . in Mexico, for example. But not infrequently the limited amount of land available to the natives and Negroes was more or less the result of a deliberate policy on the part of the whites, aimed at increasing the labour supply; examples of this having been found in the United States, South Africa and Kenya.

Where we have witnessed the occurrence of compulsory labour in colonial territories, we have seen that the representatives of the ruling class would, as a rule, form a united front against the natives. As we know, government officials often lent their assistance to the provision of labour, but this is not the only aspect of the question; for the courts too have shown a tendency to stand in support of the ruling class, treating the native with extreme arbitrariness where this might be to the advantage of their own group. . . . Because of this attitude on the part of officialdom, the native population in almost all cases lost their last chance of a certain degree of protection. The few officials who stood up for the native's rights were usually powerless to change the general situation. . . .

. . . Certain systems of compulsory labour disappeared when they no longer fulfilled their purpose (e.g., in colonial Spanish America)—only to be replaced by another system. Compulsory labour really came to an end in the first place where it was no longer necessary. This was the case in the United States, as regards the worst practices at any rate immediately after slave emancipation. For the same reason the immigration of Indian contract workers to Mauritius ceased in 1911; the Indian population of the island being so great by that time as to make further immigration unnecessary. And something similar happened in Surinam and the Dutch East Indies (Outer Provinces); after some time there was a sufficient offer of free labour in these territories, mainly because with improved labour conditions many coolies stayed on after their contract periods, thereby forming a labour reserve. Under these circumstances, contract labour under penal sanction became superfluous and was gradually abolished in 1931/1941.

In some cases, compulsory labour came to an end because of opposition from the labourers themselves, or from governments representing them; as for example the Indian Government, which in 1917 prohibited all emigration of Indians for contract labour subject to penal sanctions. For an example of the impetus toward the abolition of compulsory labour coming from the labourers themselves, we can cite what happened in the Mexico of this century. In the revolution of 1910/11, during which a start was made on the division of the large estates, an important role was played by the Indians who had till then lived to a great extent in debt bondage or a kind of serfdom. But all the same, these cases of compulsory labour coming to an end because of opposition form the exception rather than the rule, particularly when such opposition comes from the labourers themselves.

It is not easy to define the role played by ethical influences in the abolition of compulsory labour or of some of its forms. Naturally, ethics have played an important part in many decisions in this field; indeed the abolition of slavery itself was largely fought for on ethical grounds. The question, however, remains whether a ban on compulsory labour based on such grounds has much effect in actual practice. Almost always the people in the mother countries concerned have been much more open to a consideration of colonial questions from an ethical point of view than the people in the colonies as such. We have repeatedly seen how laws passed in the colonies were repealed in the mother country if they were too severe, and how the impetus toward forbidding practices which were too inhumane always seemed to come from the same source. However, all too often such a ban would be unwelcome in the colonies, and would be simply ignored; or, if necessary, the colonists would continue in their former practices a little less obviously, and, if that did not work, would resort to other methods which had the same effect in practice. In Spain, laws were continuously being passed to improve the lot of the Indian labourers, and, on paper, the encomienda system was repealed more than once. Nevertheless, this system only really came to an end when it no longer served any purpose, and even then, the subsequent position of the Indians was certainly not an improvement. More useful forms of compulsory labour would replace the repealed system. The Portuguese ruling of 1878 (when slave emancipation became a reality in the colonies) contained measures covering the protection of native rights as well—but in Africa these were simply ignored. The Dutch Government repealed penal sanction for Java after it had been in force for several years; but the planters took to other ways of enforcing compulsory labour: clauses were introduced in the labour contracts, and if the labourers did not adhere to these, they did so at their peril; debt bondage was resorted to; and unofficial assistance by the authorities did the rest. In France, public opinion was disturbed at the high death rate among those employed on the public works in Madagascar. As a result, compulsory labour for the Government was abolished—but here again, other ways were immediately provided for putting the natives to work. Public opinion in England has very often—perhaps more often than anywhere else—strongly opposed the imposition of compulsory labour; and as a result the British Government has on many occasions repealed laws drafted in the colonies. . . . [T]he most rigorous laws which were passed just after the abolition of slavery in the West Indies, in Mauritius and in the Cape Colony, were promptly rejected in London. And when in Kenya, at a much later date, all the Government officials became involved in the recruitment of labour there was such a storm of protest in England that the Government had to take action. But was there much result in the colonies? In the West Indies and in Mauritius, the Negroes could not be persuaded to work in sufficient numbers or sufficiently, and the colonies set about bringing in coolies under an indentured system which was anything but free. And in Mauritius a system of compulsory labour closely resembling that which had been banned in England came into effect later again (this time for the Indians). In Kenya, the pressure exerted by the officials on the native population to get them to work was just as great after the intervention from London—now differing only in terms of subtlety—and there were many other measures to support this pressure. In the United States, the influence of the Northern States on the Southern, accustomed to enormous resources of Negro labour, is comparable to that of a mother country on its colonial territories. The laws passed in the South shortly after the liberation of the Negroes, and aiming to keep them on the plantations, were declared unconstitutional under the influence of the North. But in reality, nothing very much changed till years later—when the situation was so far developed that the laws were no longer necessary.

Criticism from outside countries also played a role in the abolition of compulsory labour, or a particular form of it. In the Dutch East Indies an import embargo by the United States hastened the process of abolishing contract labour under penal sanction—a process which was, however, already in full swing because of the economic development of the territories. Moreover, the interference by the United States was not so much due to moral disquiet as to a fear of competition: the embargo did not apply to the import of Indian rubber, for which there was a heavy demand, but only in tobacco, which was being grown extensively in the United States itself. World-wide criticism of the state of affairs in the Portuguese colonies was probably unprejudiced by economic motives, and continued throughout the first two decades of this century, and it was more than likely under the influence of this criticism that the principle of moral and legal obligation to work was relinquished in 1928. But that which was given with one hand would seem to have been taken with the other: the "moral and legal" obligation disappeared, but there remained the moral obligation to ensure one's livelihood by means of work; officials were forbidden to recruit natives for private employers, but it remained their duty to facilitate the work of recruiting agents as much as possible; etc. Thus in effect, these changes in the Portuguese colonial laws seem to have made as little difference in practice as the reformations in the legislation of many other countries.

With the rise of the League of Nations and the institution of the United Nations Organization, action against the occurrence of compulsory labour has been taken on an international level. In the course of years various conventions were accepted prohibiting compulsory labour or, at any rate, drastically restricting it. The International Slavery Convention of 1926 drafted a resolution declaring that compulsory labour for private ends should be abolished as soon as possible, and that compulsory labour on projects of public importance should only be resorted to in the event of there being absolutely no possibility of obtaining voluntary labour. The Convention pertaining to forced labour ratified by the International Labour Conference in 1930 demanded the immediate abolition of compulsory labour for private individuals; concerning the labour imposed by an administrative body, their statement paralleled that of the previous Convention. In 1936, there was a further Convention pertaining to the recruitment of labourers; the aim being to forbid the malpractices which made labour obtained by recruitment tantamount to compulsory labour. Later there followed another Convention that declared itself to be against the use of forcible persuasion in the conclusion of labour contracts, and a convention demanding the speediest possible abolition of all penal sanctions. Nevertheless, many countries with colonies in which compulsory labour was being imposed in one form or another were very reluctant to ratify these conventions. The first-named Convention (primarily directed against slavery) was indeed ratified by 41 countries; the second by 25 countries—but of the four countries with colonies (England, the Netherlands, France and Belgium) three (the Netherlands, France and Belgium) indicated that the Convention would be applied with certain modifications. The Convention of 1936, pertaining to recruitment, has as yet only been ratified by Norway, Japan, England (1939), New Zealand, Belgium (1948) and Argentina; and the two last-mentioned conventions have only been ratified by England, New Zealand and Belgium, and by England and New Zealand respectively. We see therefore that even international conventions have not been put into practice too speedily by the governments concerned. In spite of this, the value of international action must not be underestimated. Through it certain norms at least become acknowledged by degrees, and when the economic situation is not unfavourable for the elimination of compulsory labour, measures in that direction are perhaps taken sooner than would otherwise have been the case. That the economic situation remains the determining factor even today, however, is indicated by the fact that during the slump of the thirties when far fewer labourers were required steps were often taken to abolish compulsory labour, while compulsory labour sprang into life again in many places during the war years when there was an increasing demand for man power.

## NOTES ON FURTHER READING

While there is a substantial body of literature on slavery, relatively little of it is either interpretive or comparative. The student who wishes to read further might best begin with the essay, "Slavery," by David B. Davis in *The Comparative Approach to American History* (New York, 1968), edited by C. Vann Woodward, himself a leading authority on the position of the Negro in the post-Civil War American South. Davis's *The Problem of Slavery in Western Culture*, mentioned previously, and Winthrop Jordan's *White Over Black* (Chapel Hill, N.C., 1968), are two recent, and very important, studies of the relationship between slavery and race prejudice in North America. Kenneth Stampp, in *The Peculiar Institution* (New York, 1957), has provided a close analysis of how life on the plantation actually operated, destroying the notion of the paternal slave system suggested by Ulrich Bonnell Phillips' in his *Life and Labor in the Old South* (Boston, 1927). An excellent collection of articles on *American Negro Slavery* (New York, 1968) has been edited by Allen Weinstein and Frank Otto Gatell, and Richard C. Wade, in *Slavery in the Cities* (New York, 1964), has examined the neglected area of urban slave practices.

An important debate, not represented in the present collection, is over the profitability of slavery, especially in North America. Stampp takes up the question in Chapter IX of his book, and Harold D. Woodman, in "The Profitability of Slavery: A Historical Perennial," *The Journal of Southern History*, XXIX (Aug., 1963), 303-25, reviews the arguments. Alfred H. Conrad and John R. Meyers, in "The Economics of Slavery in the Ante-Bellum South," *Journal of Political Economy*, LXVI (April, 1958), 95-130, and Eugene Genovese, "The Slave South: An Interpretation," in *Science & Society* (Dec., 1961), 320-37, present two sides of a complex debate. The problem is best summarized, however, in Hugh G. J. Aitken, ed., *Did Slavery Pay?: Readings in the Economics of Black Slavery in the United States* (Boston, 1971).

On the ancient world, Moses I. Finley has brought together the most important articles in a collection, *Slavery in Classical Antiquity: Views and Controversies* (Cambridge, 1960). An important article is "Slavery in the Ancient World," *Economic History Review*, 2nd ser., IX (1956), 185-99, by A. H. M. Jones. Dev Raj Chanana, in *Slavery in Ancient India* (New Delhi, 1960), draws upon Pali and Sanskrit sources, and Benedicte Hjejle, "Slavery and Agricultural Bondage in South India in the Nineteenth Century," *The Scandinavian Economic History Review*, XV (1967), 71-126, carries the inquiry into the last century. Isaac Mendelsohn, *Slavery in the Ancient Near East* (New York, 1949); E. G. Pulleyblank, "The Origins and Nature of Chattel Slavery in China," *Journal of the Economic and Social History of the Orient*, I (ii/1958), 185-220; and Charles Verlinden, *L'esclavage dans l'Europe médiévale* (Bruges, 1955), are standard authorities.

The debates sparked by Tannenbaum and Elkins continue. Gilberto Freyre, in *The Masters and the Slaves: A Study in the Development of Brazilian Civilization* (New York, 1946), provided a basis for Tannenbaum. Freyre's work is representative of those who use slavery as a means of examining an entire society. Other material on Brazil appears in Lewis Hanke, ed., *History of Latin American Civilization: Sources and Interpretation* (Boston, 1967), II: *The Modern Age*, pp. 155-213. The most significant work of the Brazilian school of scholars who oppose Freyre's interpretation has yet to be translated. Charles R. Boxer, in *Race Relations in the Portuguese Colonial Empire, 1415-1825* (Oxford, 1963), is closely argued. Magnus Mörner, *Race Mixture in the History of Latin America* (Boston, 1967), is brief, and Elsa V. Goveia, *Slave Society in the British Leeward Islands at the End of the Eighteenth Century* (New Haven, 1965), is a close institutional study. Slavery in Canada is examined in Robin W. Winks, *Blacks in Canada* (New Haven, 1971). For an overview of the literature, see Arnold A. Sio, "Interpretations of Slavery: The Slave Status in the Americas," *Comparative Studies in Society and History*, VII (April, 1965), 289-308.

Other areas of slavery still require much investigation. Bruno Lasker, *Human Bondage in Southeast Asia* (Chapel Hill, 1950), is a basic study. The significant new work of J. Pecírka, a Polish scholar, has yet to be translated from the German. Melville J. Herskovits, in *Dahomey: An Ancient West African Kingdom* (New York, 1938), and Bennett H. Wall, in "African Slavery," in Arthur Link and Rembert T. Patrick, eds., *Writing Southern History: Essays in Historiography in Honor of Fletcher M. Green* (Baton Rouge, 1965), approach their subject in ways not entirely accepted today. Esteban Montejo, *The Autobiography of a Runaway Slave* (London, 1968), edited by Miguel Barnet and translated by Jocasta Innes, is a fascinating Cuban document. Leonard Doob, *Becoming More Civilized* (New Haven, 1965), shows some of the problems inherent in linguistic schizophrenia as arising from conditions of subservience. Folke Dovring, "Bondage, Tenure, and Progress: Reflections on the Economics of Forced Labor," *Comparative Studies in Society and History*, VII (April, 1965), 309-23, reviews recent literature.

Excellent bibliographies may be found in Weinstein and Gatell, cited above; in the original Finley and Kloosterboer writings from which the selections presented here were taken; and in Joel Williamson, ed., *The Origins of Segregation* (Boston, 1968). New work is appearing with great frequency now, and interested readers will wish to consult *The Journal of Negro History*, *The Hispanic-American Review*, the *Journal of Southern History*, *Caribbean Studies*, *The Journal of African History*, and other scholarly periodicals. Hopefully, we may soon have translations of the more important work that has appeared in Portuguese and Spanish. Recent volumes by Carl Degler, Eugene Genovese, and Louis Ruchames are cited in the headnotes to their selections, above.

There also is a need for other collections of materials, such as the present one, to make available to student audiences the diversity of views on slavery and its effects. There are three other such books of readings to which readers of this collection may wish to turn. Richard D. Brown, *Slavery in American Society* (Boston, 1969), is limited, as its title suggests, to the New World, but within that constriction he assembles representative arguments by such scholars as Thad W. Tate, Jr., Leon F. Litwack, David B. Davis, and Winthrop D. Jordan. A fuller and more demanding collection has been edited by Eugene Genovese and Laura Foner, placing the slave societies of the Americas into a broader theoretical perspective: *Slavery in the New World: A Reader in Comparative History* (Englewood Cliffs, N.J., 1969). Patrick Richardson, in *Empire and Slavery* (New York, 1970), provides a succinct analysis of French and British slavery, in particular, with supporting documents.